ISLAMIC LAW IN SOUTHEAST ASIA

T0334815

ISLAMIC LAW IN SOUTHEAST ASIA
A STUDY OF ITS APPLICATION
IN KELANTAN AND ACEH

KAMARUZZAMAN BUSTAMAM-AHMAD

ASIAN MUSLIM ACTION NETWORK
SILKWORM BOOKS

This publication is partially funded by The Rockefeller Foundation.

Published in 2009 by
Silkworm Books
6 Sukkasem Road, T. Suthep
Chiang Mai 50200, Thailand
info@silkwormbooks.com
http://www.silkwormbooks.com

ISBN: 978-974-9511-09-1

Cover image by Julispong Chularatana

We acknowledge Bonnie Brereton for her editorial assistance.

Typeset in Warnock Pro 10 pt. by Silk Type
Printed and bound in Thailand by O. S. Printing House, Bangkok

5   4   3   2   1

FOREWORD

Problematizing views from within "Islam(s)" in Southeast Asia

In 1953 the late Gustav von Grunebaum organized a conference of leading European scholars of Islam, the first to undertake a historical and critical self-understanding of "Islamic studies." The conference examined relationships among Muslims, and between Islam and various cultures. It found that the assumptions and methods used in fields of study like Islamic history lagged a century behind those used in European history. One year later Bernard Lewis remarked that the history of the Arabs had been written primarily in Europe by historians with no knowledge of Arabic and Arabists with no knowledge of history.[1]

Half a century later, research on the subject has changed. There is an increasing number of studies on Islam written by Muslims who know the faith, the cultures, and the practices in different contexts—the works by Akbar Ahmad, Mahmoud Mumdani, Chandra Muzaffar, and Nurcholish Madjid are just a few examples among many. Also changed is the global context itself. Now perhaps more than ever, "Islam" is more than just a description of a fifteen-century-old faith shared by one-and-a-half billion people. The word has strong emotive qualities for those both within and outside the faith. Two decades ago the late Edward Said wrote, "For the right, Islam represents barbarism; for the left, medieval theocracy; for the center, a kind of distasteful exoticism. In all camps, however, there is agreement that even though little enough is known about the Islamic world there is not much to be approved of there."[2] It is therefore important to understand, from their own perspectives, the contemporary problems that Muslims are facing.

Works in this series, Islam in Southeast Asia: Views from Within, join many other writings on Islam by authors at the periphery of scholarship, using assumptions and methods that may no longer differ from those used in the centers of learning. But if such is the case, how is this series different from the other writings on Islam that are presently flooding the popular and academic landscapes?

To state the obvious, this series addresses Islam in Southeast Asia. In relation to the Islamic world, where the sacred geography, history, and language of the Middle East seems to have established that region as the center, Southeast Asia is clearly seen as the periphery. But it is misleading to conceptualize Southeast Asia as a single sociocultural entity. As is true elsewhere in the world, societies in Southeast Asia are heterogeneous. Muslims in Indonesia and Malaysia, for example, lead lives that differ from those in Thailand and the Philippines because of the different realities facing majority and minority populations in the respective countries. Furthermore, whether Muslims constitute a minority or a majority, their lives differ again when seen in contexts influenced by Javanese culture, British colonialism, Filipino Catholicism, or Theravada Buddhism, among other things. In short, the cultural topography of Southeast Asia is a rich multiplicity.

Consequently, Islam as believed in and practiced by people in the diverse worlds of Southeast Asia is not necessarily singular, since there could be as many Islams as the various contexts that constitute them.[3] The problems facing Muslims in Southeast Asia will therefore vary. Those portrayed by researchers in this series are unusual, and their analysis is at times groundbreaking, but what they underscore is that Southeast Asian Muslims struggle with multiple identities in sociocultural contexts destabilized by globalizing forces. In addition, the fact that this research is carried out by young Muslim scholars is important; the "new generation" factor could explain both the distinctive set of problems these researchers are interested in and the fresh approaches they use.

The "views from within" approach, however, is not without its own potential problems. To engage in studies claiming to be "views from within" is in some ways to guard against the study of "others" as the study of one's own self, because in such a situation writers face other types of realities that are possibly distorted in some other ways. It is therefore important for readers to appreciate the effort researchers make to situate themselves at a distance that gives them a better perspective on the social realities of their subject while retaining their sensitivity towards, and ability to relate to, the people they are studying.[4]

At a time when Islamophobia is on the rise,[5] it is essential to find fresh perspectives that will allow us to understand the new problems and tensions facing Muslims in contemporary Southeast Asian societies, and to articulate the ways in which they negotiate their lives as members of communities of faith in a fast-changing world. This series of studies by young Muslim scholars of Southeast Asia is an important step in this direction.

Chaiwat Satha-Anand
Faculty of Political Science
Thammasat University, Bangkok

Notes

1. Azim Nanji, ed., *Mapping Islamic Studies: Genealogy, Continuity and Change* (Berlin and New York: Mouton de Gruyter, 1997), xii.

2. Edward Said, *Covering Islam* (New York: Pantheon, 1981), xv.

3. Aziz Al-Azmeh, *Islams and Modernities* (London and New York: Verso, 1996).

4. I have discussed the problem of alterity in conducting research on Muslim studies in Chaiwat Satha-Anand, *The Life to this World: Negotiated Muslim Lives in Thai Society* (Singapore and New York: Marshall Cavendish, 2005), 25–26.

5. Akbar S. Ahmad, *Islam under Siege: Living Dangerously in a Post-Honor World* (Cambridge: Polity Press, 2004), 36–39.

CONTENTS

INTRODUCTION

J. N. D. Anderson in his remarkable book, *Islamic Law in the Modern World*, maintains that the legal systems of the Muslim world today can be broadly divided into three groups: (1) those that still consider *shariah* as the fundamental law and still practice it to a certain extent in their countries; (2) those that have abandoned *shariah* and become secular; and (3) those that have reached some compromise between theses two positions.[1]

In this context, it can be said that Southeast Asian states that have a Muslim majority—Malaysia, Indonesia, and Brunei Darussalam—fall into the first category, since they apply Islamic law to a certain extent. Historically, *shariah* was implemented in Southeast Asia in conjunction with local customary practices (*adat*) and/or colonial law.[2] In addition, customary practices included certain aspects of Buddhist and Hindu traditions, which had arrived several centuries earlier. In the thirteenth century, Islam came to Southeast Asia and Islamicized local traditions.[3] Islamic law developed within the region and was practiced in certain socio-cultural-political situations where it was important in unifying the Islamic kingdoms.[4]

In the fifteenth century under colonialism, Islamic law began to be replaced by colonial legal systems in the areas of commerce and trade as well as in certain political institutions, such as judiciaries and central or local administrations, to the extent that colonialism demanded.[5]

After independence, numerous Islamic groups pressured their governments to cease using colonial law and replace it with Islamic law. In Indonesia, this movement has persisted since the late 1940s when Kartosuwiryo and his allies advocated Islamic statehood for Indonesia and the use of Islamic law throughout the country.[6] In Malaysia, the 1957 constitution placed Islam firmly within the state structure, while at the same time guaranteeing religious freedom for non-Muslims.[7] Subsequently in parts of Malaysia, Islamic law has been used to replace the earlier law of the British Empire. In Indonesia, while Dutch colonial law is still used, some aspects of Islamic law are being practiced in several provinces, such as Aceh and other parts of Sumatra as well as parts of Java.

For several decades leaders in Aceh and Kelantan have urged their national governments (Indonesia and Malaysia, respectively) to allow them to implement Islam in their own province/state. In Aceh, Daud Beureueh, the most prominent Acehnese Islamic leader, demanded that Indonesian president Sukarno grant Aceh special autonomy and the right to implement Islamic law.[8] Likewise, Islamic leader Nik Aziz demanded a form of Islamic statehood for Kelantan beginning with what has come to be known as the Hudud Bill.

The struggles of Aceh and Kelantan differ from each other in their methods for achieving the right to implement Islamic law. Daud Beureueh used a radical strategy and revolted against the Sukarno regime. His efforts have been continued by the Aceh Liberation Movement (GAM), which was formerly led by Tgk. Hasan di Tiro, a descendant of Tgk. Chik Di Tiro, an Acehnese hero of the Dutch-Aceh War. By contrast, Nik Aziz's approach was nonviolent and focused on political ideas, including secession. In many ways it is similar to the platform of PAS (Parti Islam Se-Malaysia),[9] a party that seeks to implement Islamic law in Malaysia and build an Islamic state based on the Qur'an and Sunnah.[10] These efforts of PAS and Nik Aziz were successful in the October 1990 general elections, when each, in its own way, achieved the right to implement Islamic law.

Similarly, Aceh has finally achieved new status. In 1999 the Indonesian government granted Aceh "special autonomy" (*otonomi khusus*). By issuing Regulation UU 44/1999, the Indonesian government formalized the opportunity for Aceh to apply Islamic law. GAM, however, rejected this status and asked that Aceh secede from Indonesia.[11] Some have argued that granting special autonomy to Aceh Province was not the best way to solve the problem.[12] In any event, even with the effectuation of special autonomy, conflicts remain.[13] Meanwhile, the Islamic courts in Aceh have begun to enact several *qanun* (local laws/regulations).[14]

In Kelantan socio-political conflict continues between PAS, the opposition party that advocates the use of Islamic law, and UMNO (United

Malays National Organization), the government party, which opposes implementing Islamic law in Malaysia.[15] The debates on Islamic law in the national and local media show how the government's interest in eliminating PAS's influence in Kelantan and banning the implementation of Islamic law in this state and others, like Trengganu, have remarkable political resonance. The most controversial conflict was one in which PAS initiated the use of Islamic penal law in Kelantan and other states.[16] In fact, particular Islamic laws, such as one regulating the behavior of Malaysian Muslim women in the early 1990s, continue to be implemented. The Kelantan Syariah Criminal Code (II) 1993 (known as the Hudud Bill), issued in November 1993 by the State Legislative Assembly of Kelantan, has been supported by PAS as a means to enforce the implementation of Islamic law in that state. The bill is controversial, however, and remains in abeyance, still awaiting Malaysian federal government approval as of this writing. These examples demonstrate that the implementation of Islamic laws in Aceh and Kelantan represents challenging issues for the study of Islamic law in Southeast Asia. These cases are different from those in Muslim countries elsewhere, including the Middle East.[17]

There is obviously a need for a study of how and why Islamic law is being implemented in Aceh and Kelantan. The present work is intended to address these questions and others by examining how the respective governments of Indonesia and Malaysia respond to the issue of Islamic law. It also aims to fill the gaps and extend previous studies on Islamic law in Southeast Asia. For example, M. B. Hooker, a professor of Islamic law in Southeast Asia at the National University of Australia, has written many books about Islamic law in Indonesia and Malaysia,[18] but, at the time this study was written, he had never provided a detailed discussion of the current issues regarding the implementation of Islamic law in Aceh and Kelantan. Other prominent Indonesian scholars have also neglected to examine the situation in Aceh from a sociological perspective.[19] Similarly, in Malaysia, Hashim Kamali, a professor of Islamic law at the International Islamic University of Malaysia, has written many books on the subject, but has never focused on the dynamics of Islamic law in Aceh.

3

My interest in this issue emerges from my personal experience as a young scholar from Aceh and a graduate of the University of Malaysia. Challenged by the lack of studies on this subject, I was encouraged to discover the why's and how's of implementing Islamic law in Aceh, my birthplace, and in Kelantan, the place of my studies. My previous work on this issue includes articles in *Siasah* (a magazine) and *Pemikir* (a scholarly journal), which invited me to share my opinions on the controversial debate over Islamic statehood and Islamic law in Malaysia.[20] Prior to the implementation of Islamic law in Aceh, I also wrote a book summarizing my views on the issue.[21]

Research Questions and Objectives

This present study focuses on the application of Islamic law in Aceh, Indonesia and Kelantan, Malaysia. The most interesting issue concerns the dynamics of how Islamic law has been implemented in these two places thus far, and how this issue has become a source of conflict in each place. In Aceh, as we will see, the conflict between GAM and the Indonesian military (TNI) has resulted in serious impacts on the implementation of Islamic law. In Kelantan, we shall look at how the state government implements Islamic law, despite the national government's disapproval. We will also examine the methods used in the struggle to implement Islamic law in particular societies, and the extent to which socio-political and economic changes in Indonesia and Malaysia are forging the ways in which Islamic law is expressed.

The study will also analyze the dynamics involved in the implementation of Islamic law, its historical development, typologies of Islamic law, leaders' opinions regarding this issue, and government responses. In addition, various historical, political, economic, and social factors at both the national and international levels will be examined, which have significantly contributed to the movement to implement Islamic law in Kelantan and Aceh. In these ways this research will provide empirically rich analyses of how Islamic law has raised issues in particular places at specific times. As mentioned earlier, studies on Islamic law in Southeast Asia have explored numerous aspects from diverse perspectives. However, there is still a lack of research specifically focusing on the issue as it is playing out in Aceh and Kelantan. For the most part, studies have emphasized how the state governments have provided opportunities for Muslim communities to implement Islamic law in the areas of family law,[22] social dynamics,[23] *fatwa* (an official answer by a scholar to a legal question),[24] pluralism,[25] human rights,[26] gender,[27] special autonomy,[28] civil society,[29] colonialism,[30] and others.[31] Those observations have been less concerned with the application of Islamic law in Aceh and Kelantan since each is located in the periphery of its respective country and is regarded as a conflict situation. The exceptions are a small number of scholars who have written on this subject in Kelantan, such as Abdullah Alwi Haji Hassan, who provides a brief history of marriage law,[32] and Mehruj Siraj, who has studied the practice of contemporary law.[33] There has also been an investigation of the use of Islamic law in Aceh as part of a fundamentalist movement.[34]

Implementing Islamic law appears to be viewed as a way to establish an Islamic state and to apply Islamic criminal laws, including *hudud* (fixed) *qishash* (retaliation), and *ta'zir* (discretion) punishments. I am concerned with this controversial issue because in Kelantan and Aceh, Islamic statehood has not yet been realized and Islamic criminal law has not yet fully taken root. No thief has had his/her hands cut off yet, no man has been killed for illegal sexual liaisons, and so forth. There have been many hypotheses about the application of Islamic law, but few attempts to provide critical opinions. Observers always seem to assume that the implementation of Islamic law in a Muslim country resembles the situation in the Middle East. Thus, when there is a movement to implement Islamic law, it gets characterized as fundamentalist, radical, extremist, and sometimes even terrorist.[35] In Malaysia and Indonesia, however, Islamic law has been used as a resource to further political interests, and the provincial governments have, for the most part, applied only certain aspects of Islamic law, such as banking, family law, education, and so forth.[36] They have not applied the law in whole as a full substitute for the existing legal system.

This study will explore the extent of the application of Islamic law in Kelantan and Aceh, and analyze the conditions that made its emergence possible. It is important to understand the sociological implications of the law and the political causes of its emergence. Because the implementation of Islamic law is not a single narrative and cannot be separated from the histories of Malaysia and Indonesia, this study will examine the historical processes of applying Islamic law in certain states and provinces of these two countries. In addition, it will pose the question of why challenges to the existence of Islamic law are coming not only from non-Muslims, but also from the Islamic community itself. Finally, this study is intended to provide a sociological understanding of religious law as a source of both conflict and identity.

Methodology

The research conducted for this study begins with a conceptual framework that involves the meaning of Islamic law. Understanding the rise of and the perceived need to implement Islamic law is obviously central to this study. As John Strawson points out,

> One of the special characteristics of Islamic law is that it constitutes an existing system of sacred law in the contemporary world. It is in this that much juristic work needs to be done in order to understand both the role of *shari'a* within Islamic societies and its contribution to the wider international legal community. The Islamic understanding of the role of law constitutes a serious challenge to much of what we might call the Western jurisprudential lineage.[37]

The present monograph uses a social history approach, which attempts to understand the product of Islamic legal thinking in terms of its socio-cultural and socio-political contexts.[38] There are two reasons for using this approach. First, it views Islamic law in its proper position as the result of human interaction that is subject to change. Second, it might make *fuqaha* (experts in Islamic law) and *mufti* (Islamic jurists) less reluctant to make changes in Islamic law whenever necessary.[39] In this study, Islamic law is viewed as a product of human interpretation. Islamic law is then differentiated from *shariah*, as certain scholars have done elsewhere.[40] This method might be termed a sociological approach to Islamic legal studies that analyzes social and political interaction.[41]

Furthermore, this study will examine the orientation of Islamic law in Malaysia and Indonesia in order to look at its historical, political, and sociological development in Kelantan and Aceh. In so doing, it will provide numerous accounts of how Islamic law is advanced in these two places. This is important in reviewing Islamic law because it is a multifaceted issue. For instance, in the sociological context, it is significant to analyze the discourse of Islamic law in society. Does the *ummah*[42] (an Arabic word meaning "community" or "nation," specifically used to refer to the worldwide community of Muslims united by faith) really understand what Islamic law is? With regard to the historical context, the study will examine the application of Islamic law in the pre-modern Islamic kingdoms of Malaysia and Indonesia.[43] Has this historical legacy become the source of legitimating Islamic law in contemporary society? As for the political context, the study will look at the Malaysian and Indonesian governments' responses to the Islamic law issue in the specific cases of Kelantan and Aceh.

The research for this study involves both theoretical and empirical investigations. It begins with a literature review that was accomplished by visiting a number of relevant libraries and research institutes, through which books, articles, academic theses/dissertations, and research reports were obtained. The bibliographical research was completed by exploring the documentation and media coverage of Islamic law in newspapers, magazines, and the Internet. Of particular importance are publications issued by the governments of Kelantan and Aceh. A discourse analysis of speeches, informal talks, and public sermons by Islamic leaders in Kelantan and Aceh, some of which have been recorded in cassette or video-tape forms, is also included.

The fieldwork for this study included participatory observation and in-depth interviews. Participatory observation is important since the scope of this research lies in the "value domain." This method was taken in order to directly observe a variety of activities encompassing the implementation of Islamic law in Kelantan and Aceh, including social settings, cultural phenomena, and politics. All of these activities were interpreted in order to understand the meaning behind them. In-depth interviews, in particular, were employed to determine the opinions of particular key persons.

Reorientation of Islamic Law

Many books, articles, theses/dissertations, and reports seek to explain Islamic law through various languages and perspectives.[44] Here I wish to elaborate on definitions of Islamic law and issues relevant to the research topic. My main concern in this section is providing an understanding of actual Islamic law, since scholars have referred to it in various ways: *fiqh*, *shariah*, *al-ahkam al-Islamiyyah*, and Islamic jurisprudence. The debate on this issue has serious implications for realizing Islamic law as a tool in Muslims' daily life. As A. Qodri Azizy states, "many people are confused in understanding Islamic law, because they think that Islamic law is identical with the *Syari'ah* or even the *wahy* (revelation) of God."[45]

To explore this point, let us begin with the broad definition given by Joseph Schacht,[46] who describes Islamic law as

The epitome of Islamic thought, the most typical manifestation of the Islamic way of life, the core and kernel of Islam itself. The very term *fiqh*, "knowledge," shows that early Islam regarded knowledge of the sacred Law as knowledge *par excellence.*[47]

Zafar Ishaq Ansari begins his foreword with Schacht's opinion, but goes further by saying, "there can be no denying that among the world's religions, law occupies a distinctively important position in Islam, a position possibly no less important than in the religious tradition of Judaism."[48]

The position of Islamic law in Islam is very important for those who embrace this religion. Muslims are expected to learn how to apply Islamic law in daily life. According to Akh. Minhaji, it is not an exaggeration to say "there is no subject more important for students of Islam than what is usually called Islamic law."[49] Minhaji has compiled the interpretations of scholars that discussed the importance of law in Islam. First, he notes that Islam is a religion of law. Second, law is the distilled essence of the civilization of a people and since it reflects civilizations in general, there can be no doubt that this is particularly true of the world of Islam. Third, it is impossible to understand the Muslim mind, Muslim society, Muslim ideals, politics, and reactions without some knowledge of that law, which still molds and pervades them all. Moreover, law is the heart of Islam; this is a proposition that has been generally accepted within the ranks of unbelievers as well as believers, and it forms the basis of much of Islamic scholarship. For many devout Muslims, traditionalist and modernist alike, Islam without the law is unimaginable. In addition, the *shariah* was traditionally a way of life, which for Muslims constituted the core of Islam. It is, therefore, impossible to understand Islam without understanding Islamic law. Islamic law will always remain one of the most important, if not the most important, subjects of study for the student of Islam.[50]

Given the above, it can be argued that Islamic law comprises the whole of Islamic teaching. Unfortunately, when we explore what really constitutes Islamic law, we encounter many different perceptions. Earlier I raised the question, when is Islamic law considered *shariah*? When is Islamic law considered *fiqh*? Islamic law as described in Western languages has diverse interpretations, particularly according to Muslim understandings of it. As Mashood A. Baderin notes, "Islamic law, strictly speaking, is not monolithic. Its jurisprudence accommodates a pluralistic interpretation of its sources, thereby producing differences in juristic opinions that can be quite significant in a comparative legal analysis."[51]

While the terms *fiqh* and *shariah* have similar meanings, *fiqh* is used in the literal sense to mean "understanding" (*al-fahm*).[52] Basically the meaning of the term *fiqh* is usually similar to words such as *'ilm* (knowledge) and *kalam* (theology).[53] The term *'ilm* has the same meaning and, in the era of the Prophet, there appears to have been no difference between the two terms.[54] According to Imran Ahsan Khan Nyazee, "as sophistication crept in, the term *'ilm* came to be applied in a narrow sense to mean knowledge that comes through report, that is, traditions: *hadith* and *athar*. The term *fiqh* . . . came to be used exclusively for a knowledge of the law."[55] Thus the terms *'ilm* and *fiqh* were separated when specialization in law and tradition came into existence toward the end of the first century of Hijrah.[56]

Furthermore, the terms *kalam* and *fiqh* were not separated until the time of al-Ma'mun (d. AH 218). *Fiqh* until such time embraced both theological problems and legal issues.[57] That is why Abu Hanifah (d. AH 150) defined *fiqh* as *ma'rifah al-nafs ma laha wa ma 'alayha* (understanding the self in terms of one's rights and duties).[58] This means that *fiqh* concerns understanding Muslims' rights and obligations. However, when the Mu'tazilah (an Islamic theology group)[59] began to use the term *kalam* for their teaching, the term *fiqh* came to be restricted to the corpus of Islamic law. This differentiation has serious implications for the study of Islamic jurisprudence.

There are many definitions of *fiqh*. Abdul Wahhab Khallaf defines *fiqh* as "the knowledge of the legal rules pertaining to conduct that have been derived from specific evidence" (*al-'ilm bi ak-ahkam al-shayi'ah al-'amaliyyah al-muktasib min adillatiha al-tafshiliyyah*).[60] Khallaf also highlights another definition of *fiqh*, which is "the compilation of the legal rules pertaining to conduct that have been derived from specific evidence" (*majmu'at al-ahkam al-shari'ah al-'amaliyyah al-mustafadah min adillatiha al-tafshiliyyah*).[61] Abu Ishaq al-Syirazi defined *fiqh* as "the knowledge of legal rules that are derived by the process of *ijtihad*" (*ma'rifat al-ahkam al-syari'ah al-lati thariquha al-ijtihad*).[62] *Fiqh* can also be defined as a "statement concerning the understanding of the speaker of the meaning of his speech" (*'ibarah 'an fahmi gharadhi al-mutakallimun min kalamihi*).[63] It is perhaps safe to say that *fiqh* is the finding of Islamic law from the main sources (Qur'an and Sunnah) through *ijtihad*. The person who looks at the law is called *mujtahid* and this process is termed *ijtihad*. Finally, the finding of this activity is called *fiqh al-Islami* or Islamic law (*al-ahkam al-Islamiyyah*).

The term *shariah* means the source of drinking water.[64] For Arabic people, *shariah* means religion, *ath-thariqah al-mustaqimah* (the right way), and *an-nusus al-muqaddas* (sacred texts) such as the Qur'an and Sunnah.[65] Schacht says that *shariah* is "the sacred law of Islam." He goes further, noting that "[i]t is an all-embracing body of religious duties, the totality of Allah's commands that regulate the life of every Muslim in all aspects; it consists of ordinances regarding worship and ritual, as well as political and (in the narrow sense) legal rules."[66]

In other cases, scholars differentiate between *shariah* and *fiqh*. While *shariah* comes from Allah, *fiqh* is the product of human interpretation. There is only one *shariah*, while *fiqh* implies diversity. *Shariah* is authoritative, while *fiqh* is liberal, since it is a human product. Moreover, *shariah* is not subject to change; on the contrary, *fiqh* confronts many changes through socio-cultural dynamics. And finally, *shariah* is idealistic, while *fiqh* is realistic.[67]

To clarify, Islamic law is *fiqh*, not *shariah*. In this context, *fiqh*, as human interpretation, has produced Islamic law or the Islamic legal system. There are at least four types of Islamic legal literature. These include *kutub al-fiqhiyyah* (books on Islamic jurisprudence), decrees of the Islamic courts, laws and regulations by Muslim countries, and *fatwa* (legal pronouncements of a jurisconsult).[68] In this case, the application of Islamic law in Kelantan and Aceh falls into the category of laws and regulations by Muslim countries.

Moreover, the development of Islamic law, as Minhaji states, passed through three periods.[69] The first period, in the seventh century CE is usually called the formative era,[70] during which time Islamic law was very flexible and adapted itself to the local customs of societies. The second period dates from approximately the fourteenth century, when Islamic law was supposedly expounded definitively by the orthodox legal schools (i.e., Maliki, Hanafi, Syafi'i, and Hanbali), and when Muslims throughout the central Islamic lands elected to follow one of these four schools. In this era, Islamic law was considered to have become immutable. Consequently, it became increasingly rigid and static, a phenomenon that eventually resulted in the controversial notion of "the closing of the gate of creative legal reasoning" (*insidad bab al-ijtihad*).[71] This era ended at the end of the nineteenth century CE, when the Islamic nation-state began to emerge,[72] along with a growing consciousness of the need for legal reform. The third and current stage of development arose when scholars began to feel that they were unable to resolve new legal problems with the aid of classical Islamic law.[73]

To resolve legal problems in modern life, Muslims have had to reform Islamic law. Consequently, Muslim countries have broadly adopted one of three models, as noted at the outset of this study. The reformers were compelled to search for methods in which Islamic law could be interpreted, modified, and applied so as to meet the needs of modern society.[74] For the most part, Islamic law reform has been actively enacted only in the case of marriage (*al-ahwal al-syaksiyyah*) and Islamic social affairs (*mu'amalah*). According to Mudzhar, there are two broad types of Islamic law reform. The first, intra-doctrinal reform, combines many types of Islamic legal thinking. The second, extra-doctrinal reform, gives new interpretations to Islamic texts.[75]

According to Anderson, these methods of reform that are widely used in contemporary Muslim societies manifest themselves through five methods. Procedural expediency is one method that provides a much wider and more significant application to the principle of *takhsis al-qada*, the right of the ruler to define and confine the jurisdiction of the courts. Eclectic expediency, known in Arabic as *takhayyur*, is a suitable viewpoint selected from amongst various opinions in order to fulfill the needs arising from new demands of Muslim society. The third method, the expedient of re-interpretation, has been used by reformers to re-interpret the classical texts in emphasizing the importance of practicing *ijtihad*. Administrative regulation seems to be the basis for all previous methods. And, reform by juridical decision is a method by which the application of Islamic law is made by a series of judicial decisions.[76]

Understanding the position of Islamic jurisprudence within Islam and contemporary efforts to reform it, places us in a better position to examine recent developments to implement Islamic law in Kelantan and Aceh.

THE APPLICATION OF ISLAMIC LAW IN KELANTAN

Historical Context

There is still little known about the early history of Kelantan. Alexander Hamilton, who was very familiar with the Malay Archipelago in the early eighteenth century, did not even mention Kelantan in his book, *A New Account of the East Indies*.[77] Similarly, Khoo Kay Kim writes:

> One can hardly over-emphasize the importance of any historical data which have bearing on the eastern Malay states for the simple reason that these states have been unfairly [addressed in] writings which have, from time to time, appeared on these states, few are now easily accessible to the average student of Malaysian history [sic]. Moreover, the majority of the existing works tend to concentrate on development beginning from about 1900. In so far as the indigenous society itself is concerned, no careful study has been undertaken. This is no doubt due partly to the scarcity of source material.[78]

The application of Islamic law in Kelantan began when Islam came to this region in 1181.[79] The characteristics of the early period of conversion have to be contrasted with subsequent trends towards orthodoxy and rigorous application of Islamic teachings.[80] Alwi Hassan briefly explored the implementation of Islamic law in Kelantan during the years 1762–1900. The judicial system during those years was Islamic law. Hassan mentioned that by the early 1830s, a state *mufti* and a *hakim* (judge) had already been appointed. Yet the *mufti*'s role was more than a mere jurisconsult.[81]

Historically, there were four ways in which Islamic law was administered in Kelantan. First, Islamic criminal law was applied in the *shariah* court, where the *mufti* played an important role in issuing *fatwa*. Unfortunately, when Siamese-appointed British Advisor W. A. Graham came to Kelantan in 1903, he inaugurated a new administration system based on Islamic and

Malay customary principles that were already established in the state. This new administration system set up its own criminal court system, while leaving the *shariah* courts intact.[82] In the end, the British administration system not only interfered with the *shariah* courts in Kelantan, but also in other Malay federation states. British law was introduced through what was known as the "Residential System." The advice of the British administration on the enactment of specific laws was modeled on Indian legislation, which, in turn, was based on English law. The higher ranks of the judiciary were filled primarily by British or British-trained judges who naturally turned to British law whenever they were unable to find any local law to apply to new situations (particularly of a commercial character).[83]

Islamic law in Kelantan was also administered by the Majlis Agama Islam dan Istiadat Melayu Kelantan (the Council of Islamic Religion and Malay Customs of Kelantan). This body was established on December 24, 1915 and given the authority to counsel the ruler on all matters relating to Islamic religion and Malay customs.[84] The Majlis Agama played an important role in administrating Islamic affairs, such as the maintenance of mosques or other religious institutions, legal administration of Islamic education, and supervision of moral conduct in the state.[85]

The third way in which Islamic law was administered was through Islamic courts. This institution was established because the jurisdiction of *shariah* courts is very limited.[86] The Islamic courts, however, later became an integral part of the Islamic legal institution in the state. Among other things, their duties consisted of arranging and giving legal *fatwa* relating to the practice of Islam and Islamic law.[87]

Finally, Islamic law in Kelantan was administered through Islamic legal education as part of the socialization of the law to people. The development of Islamic legal studies in Kelantan began as early as the sixteenth century, and Islamic law was taught at the *pondok* (religious boarding schools).[88] Hassan has given a vivid description of a typical *pondok:*

The *pondok* school is situated in an area of several acres of land. Located in the middle of this land is a big wooden house belonging to the principal teacher (called Tok Guru) and a few similar houses for the assistant teachers. A *madrasah* or *balaisah* (a prayer house smaller than a *surau*) is sited next to the house of the assistant teachers. The houses and the *madrasah* are surrounded by *pondok* for male students. Most students who attend the *pondok* schools are those who completed basic religious lessons in their own villages, states, or countries. In every *pondok*, besides the principal teacher, there are two or more assistant teachers, who are usually graduates of that particular *pondok*. The assistant teachers . . . are assisted by tutors known as *kepala mutala'ah*, who teach newcomers, whether elementary or intermediate, lessons. The tutors, being senior students, are normally taught advanced lessons by the principal teacher twice or more than twice a week. The tutors are also allowed to teach at other nearby locations or villages on weekends.[89]

It is believed that the education system adopted by the *pondok* was the Haramayn and University of al-Azhar model.[90] In Kelantan the *pondok* have played an important role in society. Most of its teachers were Mecca alumni. From the end of the nineteenth century up until World War II, Kelantan was known as Serambi Mekkah (the Verandah of Mecca) because many Kelantan *ulama* (religious scholars), such as Tuan Tabal (1819–1891), Haji Wan Ali Abdul Rahman Kutan (1937–1912), and Haji Yakob bin Haji Abdul Halim, were Masjidil Haram alumni.[91]

Besides the *pondok*, there is another type of Islamic legal educational institution known as the religious school, of which there are two types in the state: the *majlis* schools and the people's religious schools. The *majlis* schools were inaugurated on August 5, 1917 under the name al-Madrasah al-Muhammadiyahal-Kelantaniyyah.[92] The *madrasa* (Islamic school)[93] were established with three divisions: religious schools, which were operated by the *majlis* and located in the capital mosque; Malay schools, which were also a form of Malay religious schools; and British schools.[94] The people's religious schools (*sekolah-sekolah ugama rakyat*), which were numerous in Kelantan, were responsible for producing Islamic legal education and experts. However, since these were primary and secondary schools, they could not fulfill higher expectations and were only feeders to other Islamic institutes of higher learning in the state and abroad. Nevertheless, they played an important role in the development of Islamic legal education in Kelantan.[95]

Political Context

Generally speaking, the political situation in Malaysia has always been dominated by Malay people. It is well acknowledged that the discourse of Malaysia also includes Islam both politically and sociologically. In other words, the politicization of Islam has become a key factor in the Malaysian political terrain in recent years, and has found dominant expression in the so-called Islamization race between UMNO and PAS.[96] PAS's history goes back to its establishment on November 24, 1954. Dominated by *ulama* from Al-Azhar and Haramayn,[97] this party aimed at implementing Islamic law and Islamic statehood based on the Qur'an and Sunnah.[98] Political Islam has, for some time, manifested itself in great intra-communal tension within the Malay community. As the two Malay political parties battle for political legitimacy and electoral support, the resulting competition has led to efforts to institutionalize Islam and expand the religious bureaucracy, thereby sharpening the debate over what Islam means in Malaysia and how it should be practiced.[99]

There are two problems about how to situate Islam in Malaysia. The first is the question of the relationship between Islam and the state, which because it has never been satisfactorily resolved by Islamic thinkers continues to play a vital role in the ongoing debate. The second is the shift in meaning of Islamic debates that has mostly been overlooked in a perspective too narrowly focused on Islam as a united political and social force.[100]

These two problems demonstrate the important role played by the

Malay people in Malaysia. The most representative Islamic figures are from Malay parties such as PAS and UMNO. From those elite parties we get information about the political context that has affected the issue of implementing Islamic teachings in Malaysia. PAS provides an interesting example with its attempt at constructing and enforcing a system of "Islamic democracy" in the two east coast states of Kelantan and Trengganu.[101] Joseph Liow maintains that "driven by the global resurgence of Islamic consciousness and strengthened by the enthusiasm of the new guard epitomized by the likes of Fadzil Noor, Abdul Hadi Awang, and Nakhaie Ahmad, a rejuvenated PAS began pushing a more deliberate Islamic agenda in Malaysia to whittle away support for UMNO."[102]

Within UMNO, there is also debate on how to situate Islam in modern Malaysia. Basically, the roots of the controversy among UMNO's members involve the question of how Malaysia can be both modern and Islamic. The real debate has been over interpretation of the *shariah*, especially after Anwar Ibrahim first joined the party. He integrated the struggle for socio-economic justice with Islamic ideals, thus using this philosophy to organize students behind him in the campaign against pro-Western leaders.[103]

This step has been interpreted as an attempt by former Prime Minister Mahathir Mohammad to weaken the Islamic opposition while at the same time strengthening the government's Islamic credentials.[104] This dilemma has serious implications for UMNO in its election strategy because most Malay people are Muslim and almost all Muslims in Malaysia are Malay. The problem of identity becomes a source of debate within UMNO itself.

Under Mahathir, Islam was brought to the forefront of UMNO and Malaysian politics. Many of Mahathir's ideas were adopted by the government and UMNO. He criticized PAS as an opposition party that is not interested in Malaysia's development. UMNO has resorted to controlling the mainstream media to generate public apprehension regarding the Islamic opposition. In an attempt to define the boundaries of Islamic politics in Malaysia, the UMNO-led government regularly portrays PAS members as "fanatics" and "radicals" while portraying its own as representatives of "modern" and "progressive" Islam. Consequently, provocative remarks purportedly made by PAS leaders over the years and amplified by the government-controlled media have further promoted negative images of PAS fundamentalism.[105]

Mahathir's vision of Islam as a force for modernization and industrialization reportedly won high acceptance from most non-Muslim Malaysians. The majority of Muslim Malaysians, however, do not agree with this vision,[106] because it seems to give special rights to non-Malays, particularly in the economy. Accordingly, "Malay people now want to pressure the government to give special rights to Muslims by bringing back Malay culture with Islamic coloring."[107]

By 1999 the tensions had become stronger when PAS extended its political control beyond the northeastern state of Kelantan to Trengganu in the election and became the main voice of the opposition.[108] The issues of Islamic statehood, the implementation of *shariah*, and the role of women have brought the two parties into acrimonious debate. In September 2001, Mahathir declared that Malaysia was an "Islamic state." According to Zainah Anwar, a gender expert and executive director of SIS (Sisters in Islam), an Islamic liberal activist group in Malaysia, this declaration was unconstitutional because it was not issued formally as a new law.[109]

On June 18, 2002, Mahathir went so far as to say that Malaysia is an Islamic fundamentalist state and can be proud of the fact. The Malaysian government's policies, he said, abide by the fundamental teachings of Islam.[110] He acknowledged that his views would shock many in the West because they consider a fundamentalist to be "someone who is violent and does all kinds of bad things." But he said this perception was wrong and, furthermore, it is not necessarily a bad thing to be a fundamentalist.

PAS, however, declared that Malaysia should be an Islamic state in law as well as in practice and introduced this concept in Kelantan and Trengganu. Through its "Islamic State Document," PAS promoted the establishment of Islamic statehood arguing, among other things, that Islamic political leadership is an important institution necessary for the achievement of human progress. Moreover, the implementation of Islam as a comprehensive way life should be realized through the establishment of an Islamic state based on the guiding principles of the Qu'ran and Sunnah as well as provisions of the *shariah*. In committing itself both to the interests of religion and the nation, PAS proposes "to struggle for the establishment of a society and government in this country that embodies and manifests Islamic values and laws that seek the pleasure of the Almighty." [111]

In order to convince Malaysians to support the implementation of Islamic law, PAS put forth a number of reasons why *hudud* (one of four categories of punishment under Islamic Penal Law) should be enforced pursuant to the Kelantan Syariah Criminal Bill (II) of 1993. According to PAS:

- *Hudud* law is God's law and this is stated in the Qur'an[112]
- Muslims have no choice but to accept *hudud*[113]
- Man-made laws have loopholes
- Crimes of all types are becoming more serious
- Those who question the law are not necessarily bad Muslims, but they are merely ill-informed
- Those who reject the laws are apostates
- *Hudud* laws are only meant for Muslims
- The law will make everyone safe
- Non-Muslims will see the value of implementing *hudud* laws because they protect the public, prevent crimes, and provide just punishment for convicted persons.
- *Hudud* law should be implemented even though the majority of people do not fully understand the law.[114]

It is safe to say that the issue of Islamic law in Malaysia serves the political interests of both PAS and UMNO. I would argue that the political arena in Malaysia still faces the same issues and controversies regarding political Islam as in other Muslim communities, including the establishment of

Islamic statehood and Islamic law. In most of the Muslim world these two issues have serious implications for both Muslims and non-Muslims. Malaysia's case, in some ways, is the same as those of other countries, such as Indonesia, Sudan, Pakistan, Egypt and so forth. As Jan Stark of Universiti Sains Malaysia has observed, since the fall of communism a new world order is emerging in which political Islam is developing into one of the major players. Islam not only provides new stimuli for the re-definition of political models and social and cultural identity, it also views globalization as one of its outspoken critics.[115]

The Hudud Bill

The most controversial issue of attempting to implement Islamic law in Malaysia is the Kelantan Syariah Criminal Bill (II) 1993, colloquially referred to as the "Hudud Bill." This measure was inaugurated unanimously by all thirty-six state assemblymen in Kelantan, including two from the Barisan Nasional (BN) party. It was supported and issued by PAS, the victorious party in Kelantan during the 1990 election.

The Hudud Bill primarily consists of provisions for implementing *hudud*, *qishas*, evidence, and punishment in Kelantan. In Part I of the bill, the types of *hudud* offences mentioned are *sariqah* (theft), which consists of removing property by stealth from the possession of its owner without his consent; *hirabah*, taking another person's property by force or threat of force by a person or persons armed with a weapon or other object capable of being used as a weapon; *zina* or sexual intercourse between a man and a woman who are not married to each other; *qazaf*, an accusation of *zina* that cannot be proved by four witnesses against a competent adult Muslim who is known to be chaste; *shurb* or consuming any intoxicating drink by any person, whether intoxicated or not; and *irtidad*, any word uttered by a Muslim which affects or is against the belief in Islam. Some of these offenses are punishable by whipping, others by amputating hands or feet, and still others by stoning.

Part II of the bill focuses on *qisas* and *diyat*. Both terms refer to homicide and causing bodily injury. Homicide is divided into three categories: (a) willful killing; (b) quasi-willful killing; and (c) killing without intention. Part III discusses the evidence of *hudud* and *qisas*. Many issues arise from this part of the bill, namely how to prove an offence, the number of witnesses required, qualifications of witnesses, nature of the testimony, withdrawal of testimony, retraction of confession, and circumstantial evidence. This section of the bill resembles the discussions of *fiqh* in Islamic legal studies regarding *jarimah hudud* (fixed punishments) and *tazir* (punishment at the discretion of a judge).[116] But in clause 46(3), it is stated that *tazir* is an alternative punishment to *hudud* where the evidence does not fulfill the conditions required to prove a *hudud* offence.

In Part IV, the bill examines how punishments are carried out. It is stated that *hudud* punishment imposed under this enactment shall not be suspended, substituted for any other punishment, reduced, pardoned, or otherwise altered. The bill specifies that there should be a medical checkup before any punishment is carried out. If the offender faces several offences, the punishment will be carried out in the following ways: (a) if the punishments are of the same kind and graveness, only one punishment shall be carried out; (b) if the punishments are the same kind, but of different graveness, only the severest punishment shall be carried out; (c) if the punishments are different kinds, all shall be carried out; (d) if one of the punishments is death all other punishments shall be set aside.

Part V includes general provisions. Clause 62(1) states that all offences under this enactment and related provisions shall be interpreted according to *shariah* law and precedents. Moreover, clause 62(2) states that the court trying the case shall have jurisdiction to give meaning to such word, expression, or term if any doubt or difficulty arises in the interpretation of any word, expression, or term relating to *shariah* law.

The bill also delineates the courts responsible for implementing *shariah* law in Kelantan: a special Syariah trial court with jurisdiction over offences under the enactment of the bill and a special court of appeals to hear appeals from the decisions of the special Syariah trial court.

The Controversy over the Bill

When the bill was issued in 1993, there were many responses from the elite, *ulama*, academia, NGO activists, and non-Muslims. Mahathir, who was prime minister at the time, was against it, claiming that the law was the result of PAS's own understanding and interpretations of the Qur'an. He also argued that it was politically motivated.[117] In Mahathir's words, the PAS-proposed law was not the result of a valid *ijtihad* process; it was produced to serve other than Islam and was spurred by PAS's political motives. PAS itself admitted that this law was created because of political pressure from UMNO. However, it was not motivated by Islamic politics, which is different.[118]

Mahathir maintained that the federal government of Malaysia, as a democratic country, would allow the implementation of *hudud* laws.[119] However, he raised two questions to challenge the PAS proposal. First, was this law indeed created in accordance with Islamic jurisprudence, i.e., based on *fiqh*? In brief, the answer is no. The *ulama* in the country, even in Kelantan, did not participate in the process that gave birth to the law. Second, can the law guarantee justice for all who are indicted under it? Supporters contend that *hudud* law does not stress the severity of the sentence, but rather ensures that justice is done.[120] Detractors disagree.

Non-Muslim political elites rejected the PAS law in Kelantan. DAP (Democratic Action Party) reportedly opposed the imposition of Muslim laws on non-Muslims in any state, including the *hudud* laws that carry penalties of limb amputation, whipping, and stoning. Lim Kit Siang, DAP secretary-general, said the imposition of such laws by the state or federal government was against the country's constitution and this applies to the PAS-led Kelantan state government.[121] Yet in 1999, PAS and DAP collaborated with Barisan Alternatif and other parties in Malaysia.[122] Barisan Alternatif (Alternative Front) was running against Barisan Nasional (National Front), the coalition party under which UMNO operates. But because of *hudud* and the Islamic state issue, DAP withdrew from Barisan

Alterntif, since PAS wanted to implement Islamic law not only in Kelantan, but also in Trengganu.[123]

Most scholars in Malaysia also opposed the bill. Mohammed Hashim Kamali, a prominent professor of law at the International Islamic University Malaysia, has described some of the defects of the Hudud Bill, including those related to procedural, jurisdictional, and constitutional matters.

> First, there are problems involving the realities of Malaysian society and politics. In the context of a multi-religious society, this bill raises questions as to whether the nation should be governed by two sets of laws, one for Muslims, another for non-Muslims. Second, only one of the thirteen states of Malaysia has charted a different plan for itself and has consequently confronted the national government with difficult choices. Third, the bill fails to offer a meaningful alternative as it raises questions over the wisdom of a literalist approach to the understanding of *hudud*. The bill exhibits no attempt to exercise *ijtihad* over new issues, such that would fulfill the ideals of justice and encourage the development of a judicious social policy.[124]

Kamali raises many issues regarding misinterpretations of the PAS-initiated bill. According to him, the bill is a product of undiluted imitation (*taqlid*) that fails to acknowledge the contemporary realities of society and fails to make necessary adjustments to some of the *fiqhi* formulations of premodern times.[125] His conclusion is based on his study of the discourses of *hudud* in the Qur'an, Sunnah, and Fiqh.

Sisters in Islam contends that the bill discriminates against Malaysian women in several ways, including the grounds for presumption of *zina*; the disqualification of women as eye-witnesses; the determination of a marriage by a husband's accusation of *zina* (*al-lian*), whether proved or not, against his wife; and the implied endorsement of the view that *diyat*, or compensation for death or injury, to a women should be half that for a man.[126] In November 1993 the group held a forum to critique the bill. Speakers and participants in that forum were generally critical of it. In their view the bill exhibited gender bias against women.[127] Salbiah

Ahmad, a member of SIS, has written about myriad other ways the bill discriminates against women.[128]

The Hudud Bill has not yet been approved by the Malaysian federal government and its legislature. In governing the state, PAS had to negotiate the various obstacles that stood in its way of establishing an Islamic government based on *shariah*. In the long run, it could not introduce policies that were not supported by the majority of non-Malays or the more secularized urban Malay middle-class voters. The 1993 *hudud* controversy underlined another check on PAS's prerogative as a state government. PAS could not propose a law that violated the federal constitution and federal government, nor could it risk being cut off from government funds if it openly defied the Malaysian political structure.[129]

Even so, the attempt by the PAS-controlled government in Kelantan to impose the Hudud Bill is still seen by many Muslim women as a serious threat to their rights and status.[130] While many women's organizations have challenged the bill in Malaysia, a problem arises over who has the authority to speak about Islam. Zaenah Anwar, SIS executive director, says that when women's groups and lay intellectuals speak about Islam, their credentials and their rights and authority to speak publicly are questioned.[131]

The other troublesome impact of the attempt to implement Islamic law in Kelantan is the narrow interpretation of the law. For instance, the provision in the PAS *hudud* law that women cannot be witnesses is only a juristic opinion with no explicit support in the Qur'an or traditions of the Prophet Muhammad. Moreover, in Islamic legal studies there are four *mazhab* (schools of Islamic legal thought: Hanafy, Maliki, Shafi'i, and Hanbali) that can be used by Muslims anywhere in the world. Pregnancy as evidence for *zina* is a minority position of the Maliki school of law. The majority *shariah* opinion is that pregnancy is not admissible as proof of *zina* because circumstantial evidence cannot be accepted to secure a *hudud* punishment. And yet PAS ideologues in Malaysia, who belong to the Shafi'i school, chose to ignore the more enlightened opinion of the majority and instead codified the harsher Maliki opinion. But when a

Maliki or Hanbali opinion is more advantageous to women, certain PAS members would proclaim that this is unacceptable, arguing, "We are Shafiites and we must follow Shafi'i rulings."[132]

A further issue is that PAS, after gaining control of Kelantan, promoted the program "Development Together with Islam" (Membangun Bersama Islam) in an attempt to strengthen the role of Islam in both politics and economics.[133] This concept is based on three principles: *itqan* (ability), *ubudiah* (submission), and *mas'uliah* (responsibility). According to Jan Stark, "PAS intends to implement *shariah* as an alternative socio-economic model which replaces the capitalist system with a more balanced approach giving priority to the role of man in a more spiritual and just society."[134]

However, it is obvious that the Islamic concept brought by PAS to Kelantan did not benefit the local people in any way. Kelantan is reportedly the poorest state in Malaysia and the people are still waiting for help from the federal government. But since the national government party was victorious in the 2004 election in Kelantan, the Islamic government that was established by PAS in Kelantan did not receive any support from the Malaysian national government. And, although PAS made great strides in the 2008 elections, it saw some of its support erode in the recent 2009 by-elections.

Federal projects in Kelantan have sought to improve infrastructure, especially overcoming the development gap between the southern and northern parts of the state. However, since these are federal projects carried out as part of national planning—the Eighth Malaysia Development Plan (Rancangan Malaysia Kelapan)—and handled by the federal works agency, Jabatan Pembangunan Persekutuan (JPP), PAS has only limited control. For instance, government tenders are generally given to the private sector, which is largely dominated by corporate construction companies, thus giving PAS little say in choosing contractors that conform to the party's principle of shared benefits (*maslaha*).[135]

On social and cultural levels, PAS has, since 1993, promoted the "Islamic public sphere" or "Islamic face," by which nightclubs and all establishments serving alcohol would be restricted by the local administration on the grounds that they encouraged drinking, dancing, close proximity between men and women, and "unruly, unrestrained behaviour."[136] Because of this rule, non-Muslims in Kelantan do not support PAS. In promoting *hudud* as a vital means to establish inter-ethnic, inter-religious solidarity and equality through the application of Islamic jurisdiction for all, PAS has to reassure non-Muslims that they will be exempted from its laws if it wants to alleviate their concerns about the implementation of Islamic law.[137]

THE APPLICATION OF ISLAMIC LAW IN ACEH

Nanggroe Aceh Darussalam is located in the northern part of Sumatra, or in the western-most part of the archipelago of 17,000 islands that comprise Indonesia. It covers an area of 57,365,57 square kilometers, with a population of 3.929 million. The breakdown by religious affiliation is Muslims (97 percent), Christians (2.3 percent), Hindus (0.01 percent), Buddhists (0.37 percent), and others (0.02 percent). The most densely populated area is Banda Aceh, while West Aceh is sparsely populated. Aceh is also home to numerous ethnic groups.

Rich in oil and natural gas, Aceh accounts for 13 percent of Indonesia's oil production. The P. T. Arun oil fields generate 4 million dollars a day, nearly all of which goes to Jakarta. Its qualified natural gas is partly owned by Mobil Oil Corporation (35 percent), and partly by the Indonesian state company Pertamina (55 percent). Aceh is also said to be the second largest producer of marijuana in Southeast Asia, which is almost entirely for export; all sides of the armed conflict are said to be involved in this trade.[138]

Over the course of Aceh's history, interaction with Indians, Chinese, Arabs, and Europeans has brought about lasting influences not only in terms of culture but also in the physical appearance of the people. Traveling through this region one encounters a wide variety of cultures and traditions. Many Acehnese customs were adopted from Indian and Arab traditions. Similar to Kelantan, Aceh is a major gateway of Islamic studies in Southeast Asia and is known as the Serambi Mekkah (Verandah of Mecca) in Indonesia.[139] The process of Islamization in Aceh is important to understand because it sheds light on the position of Islam in Southeast Asia in general, and Indonesia in particular.[140]

There are many theories about the coming of Islam to Aceh. Most scholars agree that it arrived, not in the thirteenth century CE from Gujarat, but as early as the seventh century CE from Saudi Arabia.[141] Karel A. Steenbrink, an Indonesianist from the Netherlands who has written several books, claims that before the thirteenth century CE many "Muslims came to Indonesia" and "Indonesians embraced Islam."[142] According to this source, prior to the thirteenth century most Acehnese had already become Muslim through contact with travelers from the Middle East and South Asia.

There are many reasons why the spread of Islam became noticeable in and around Aceh. According to Yusny Saby, Arab merchants happened to control the trade routes in the Indian Ocean long before the birth of the Prophet, and thus they facilitated the spread of Islam later. Personal contacts also played an important role in the Islamization process.[143] In Aceh many Arab travelers married Acehnese women. In this way contact with the indigenous population became even closer.[144] However, Atho Mudzhar argues that although visiting Arab, Persian, and Indian merchants played a crucial role in commercial relations, their contribution to the introduction of Islam in the region was limited.[145] In his opinion, the actual dissemination of Islam among the local people and their mass conversion to Islam was due to the untiring efforts of Indian preachers, particularly Bengali Sufis (mystics), who accompanied the merchants on their visits to the local rulers.[146]

Aceh attracted traders from East and West interested in its pepper and other spices. In addition, its sultans' patronage of religious teachings caused the court to be surrounded by learned scholars, who played an important role in Aceh, especially in the Islamic kingdoms.[147] Historically, the *ulama* in Aceh always acted as advisors for the rulers in the role of *mufti* or *qadhi malikul aadil* (a scholar that interprets or expounds Islamic law). In 1582 CE two scholars from Mecca reportedly arrived in Aceh, and at about the same time there came from Gujarat one Shaykh Muhammad Jaylani, a popular teacher of logic, rhetoric, and jurisprudence. To meet the demand for guidance in mysticism, he spent several years studying in Mecca, returning to Aceh later.[148] In *Bustan al-Salatin*, Nurdin al-Raniri, one of the leading *ulama* from India, tells a slightly different version of the story in which the arrival of Islam occurred not in 1582 CE, but in 1580 CE, and the names of the scholars who brought the religious teachings are Shaykh Abu al-Khayr

Ibn Hajar and Shaykh Muhammad Yamani. The former was the author of *Al-Sayf al-Qati*, a book on Sufi thought that discusses the problematic nature of the third metaphysical category between being and non-being, known as the fixed essences. Shaykh Muhammad al-Yamani taught the science of the sources (*al-ushul*), that is, the sciences relating to the Holy Qur'an, the usage of the Holy Prophet (*al-sunnah*), the consensus of opinion or agreement (*al-ijma*), and the traditions relating to the Prophet's companions (*al-athar*).[149]

It should be pointed out that in Aceh Islamic teaching was limited to Sufism issues and serious implications of Islamic thought. Consequently, before Nurdin Al-Raniri came to Aceh, the most prominent issues still involved mysticism. The *ulama* in Aceh concerned with Sufism were Hamzah Fansuri (1550–1600 CE) and Syamsuddin As-Sumatrani (d. 1629 CE).[150] The former, who lived in Barus on the west coast of northern Sumatra was said to be the greatest Malay Sufi poet and the first man to translate Sufi doctrines and metaphysics into Malay. The latter was his probable disciple, and became the Shaykh al-Islam of Aceh, who advised the sultan on religious and cultural matters and also acted on his behalf in diplomatic and international affairs.[151] When Nurdin al-Raniri returned to Aceh in 1637, the Sultanate of Iskandar Thani appointed him as the Shaykh al-Islam. Since Nurdin al-Raniri was against the doctrine of *wujudiyyah*, he advised the sultan to burn the works of the Sufi *ulama* Hamzah Fansuri.[152]

In the seventeenth century CE, four queens in succession reigned over Aceh, and in the eighteenth century sultans of Arab blood (Sayyid) came to the throne.[153] Before their reign (1607–1637 CE), Aceh was ruled by Sultan Iskandar Muda, a vigorous and conquering ruler who subjugated many kingdoms, including Deli (1610 CE), Johore (1613 CE), Pahang (1616 CE), Kedah (1619 CE), Perak (1620 CE), Nias (1624 CE), and attempted a reconquest of Malacca (1626 CE).[154] Iskandar Muda is credited with bringing Islamic reforms to Aceh, and promulgating statutes that would make Aceh an Islamic state.[155] In addition, he also attached himself and his kingdom to the consultation of the *ulama*.[156]

The collaboration between *ulama* and rulers implies the implementation of Islamic law since the sultans appointed *ulama* to be the *mufti* or *qadhi malikul adil*. Hamzah Fansuri served Sultan 'Ala al-Din Ri'ayat Shah Sayyid Mukammal (1588–1604 CE). Shamsuddin al-Sumatrani served at the court of Sultan Iskandar Muda until his death. Nurdin al-Raniri, during his tenure at the Acehnese court, also functioned as the political advisor to the ruler Sultan Iskandar Muda.

Nurdin al-Raniri was the first *'alim* at the court to give a *fatwa* on the legitimacy of women as rulers. As Saby points out, Nurdin "defended his position vigourously against the opposition of the *ulama* of the Hijaz, to whom the most crucial religious problems were referred. Nurdin's stand on this matter is historic, yet it remains controversial."[157]

Another scholar that had an important impact on Islamic teaching in Aceh is Abdur Rauf Singkel, who was appointed as *qadhi* by Sultan Taj al-'Alam Safiyatuddin Shah. He dedicated his book on Islamic jurisprudence to the sultan, which was entitled *Mir'at Tullab*.[158] He also served the court and validated the *shariah* ruling regarding the legitimacy of female rulers in Aceh. Without his approval, female succession could have been jeopardized.[159] However, in the sixteenth century the *mufti* of Mecca, in the name of Islamic law and orthodoxy, issued a *fatwa* that forbade women from attaining the position of sultan.[160]

It is safe to say that the *ulama* of the Aceh sultanate regarded themselves as free to interpret the *shariah* according to their own assessment of the needs of the time and the particular situation.[161] The Mecca intervention through the *fatwa* did, however, rigidified Islamic legal thought in Aceh. The polemic in Aceh was not based on Islamic teaching, but only on political interests. It was apparent to most that such a *fatwa* could have been issued while Abdur Rauf Singkel was in office, but those who opposed having women as rulers appeared to have waited for his death, and then they acted promptly.[162]

The *ulama*, besides serving as *mufti* or *qadhi malikul adil*, also wrote many books. The first book on *fiqh* in Indonesia, *Sirat al-Mustaqim*, was written by Nurdin al-Raniri,[163] at the request of Sultan Iskandar Sani who wanted the Acehnese people to know about Islamic law. Composed in Malay, this work was begun in 1634 and completed seven years later. It deals with the science of practical judgments pertaining to religious practice (*fiqh*), but treats only those aspects concerned with devotional duties (*al-'ibadat*). Practical duties (*al-mu'amalat*) were treated later by 'Abdur Rauf Singkeli (d. 1639 CE) in his *Mir'at al-Tullab*. The *Sabil al-Muhtadin* by Muhammad Arshad al-Banjari was written in 1892 on much of the same topics as al-Raniri's book but in a more accessible fashion, and was reprinted many times.[164]

The *Mir'at al-Tullab*, according to Azyumardi Azra, "is the first book in Malay-Indonesian dealing with *Fiqh Mu'amalat* and concerning social, political, economic, and religious aspects of Muslim life."[165] There is also a book of *fiqh* that includes a compilation of *fatwa* entitled *Muhimmat al-Nafa'is fi bayan as'ilat al-hadith* (Precious Gems Explaining Questions About Current Topics). According to B. J. O. Schrieke, this book is an Arabic Malay collection of *fatwa* published in Mecca in 1912 by the Acehnese 'Abd al-Salam ibn Idris. It discusses the issues submitted by Indonesians to the authority of the Meccan experts during the previous half century.[166]

During the early seventeenth century many Acehnese went to Mecca both to perform the *hajj* and to study. As a result, the Haramayn connection became important for Acehnese people. Anyone who studied in Mecca went back to Aceh to teach at the *dayah* (Acehnese Koranic schools),[167] where students learned Islamic teachings, especially Islamic law. They eventually became the *ulama* in the archipelago.

For centuries the *ulama* of Aceh have obtained their knowledge of religion from traditional religious schools, known as *meunasah rangkang bale* (small places in villages for studying Islam).

Shariah and *Adat* Law

Generally, in Aceh, the people believe that *adat* (traditional customary practices) and *shariah* should take their place side by side one another.[168] C. Snouck Hurgronje quotes Acehnese proverbs that say, "*Hukum* and *adat* are inseparable, just as God's essence and his attributes are inseparable," and "*Hukum* and *adat* are like the pupil and the white of the eye; the *hukum* is Allah's *hukum* and the *adat* Allah's *adat*."[169]

In Acehnese society, *adat* is seen as a way to understand and to implement *shariah*.[170] Before the coming of Islam, the Acehnese were influenced by Hinduism and Buddhism.[171] After Islam arrived in the region, it replaced these traditions with Islamic teachings. The *adat* that control the lives of Muslims in other parts of the Islamic world, such as the Bedouins of Arabia, the Egyptians, the Syrians, and the Turks, for example, are, for the most part, different from those of the Acehnese, Indonesians, and Malays. The relationship of these local traditional practices to the law of Islam, however, and the tenacity with which they maintain themselves, are similar.[172]

Adat plays an important role in Acehnese society. The administration of the *kampung* (village) is ruled by the *adat* system based on *shariah*.[173] The *kampung* is administered by three offices, namely, the *keuchik*, the *teungku*, and the *ureung tuha*. The *keuchik* is the headman, and the Acehnese at one time called him "the father of the *kampung*."[174] The *teungku* is seen as "the mother of the *kampung*."[175] Mukti Ali states that although the *keuchik* devotes himself more particularly to maintaining the *adat*, the promotion of "godly living" among his people is also regarded as part of his duty. The upholding of the *hukum* (law) is the *teungku*'s specialty, although a knowledge of and regard for the *adat* are also regarded as indispensable.[176] The *ureung tuha*, which is the equivalent of "elders," are the men of experience, worldly wisdom, good manners, and knowledge of *adat* in the *kampung*. They are generally persons who have reached a certain age, but a younger man who displays these characteristics is equally eligible to be an *ureung tuha*.[177]

In daily life, these leaders work together in many ways according to Islamic teachings. The center of their activities is the *meunasa* (Ar. *madrasa*), which is the place of prayer and also Islamic education.[178] The *meunasa* also serves as a place to sleep for the men in the area, a rest house for strangers, and a place to assemble on special occasions. It is there that the affairs of the *kampung* are debated, village festivals held, contracts of marriage concluded, and so forth.[179]

It is safe to say that *shariah* and *adat* in Aceh are in harmony with one another, since all Acehnese people believe *adat* is part of *shariah*. This system only became subject to question after the Dutch colonized Aceh and introduced their own administration system, supplanting local traditional practices. Dutch scholars, like Hurgronje, maintain that *adat* should be separated from *shariah* because *adat* belongs to *ulee balang* or *umara* (leaders) and *shariah* belongs to the *ulama*. The Dutch, in fact, promoted *adat* while at the same time tried to eliminate the institutionalization of Islamic values.[180] As a result, the Dutch paid attention only to the *ulee balang*, not to the *ulama*. The consequence of this strategy is that *shariah* is seen as different from *adat*.

The Nature of the Conflict

The application of Islamic law in Aceh before the European colonialists came was proceeding well. After the Europeans arrived, they substituted their law for the traditional and legal system in Aceh. The Portuguese entered Aceh with the mission of spreading Christianity in the archipelago. However, according to Lutfhi Auni, the religious response of the Acehnese to the Portuguese is difficult to ascertain since there is no single work by the *ulama* of Aceh during the sixteenth century on that matter.[181] Once the Dutch arrived in Aceh, Islamic law and the discourse of Islamic teachings came into question. Hurgronje writes:

At the time of the coming of the Dutch to Aceh there were numerous schools throughout the country; and it is a notorious fact that on more than one occasion the students from these schools threw themselves, practically unarmed, upon the bayonets of the Dutch troops. These were youths inflamed to fanaticism by the teaching they had imbibed in regard to the holy war and the reboundless recompence in the hereafter awaiting the martyr to his creed, without his being called on to render further account of his actions in this world. In estimating their contempt for death, however, we must reflect upon the fact that at that time the most fearful rumours were current in Acheh as to the tortures which would be the lot of anyone who fell alive into the hands of the *kafirs*.[182]

In his "theory of *receptie*," Hurgronje argues that Islamic law could only be effective and binding upon Indonesian Muslims if it were consistent with or derived from customary practices, the *adat*. For Hurgronje, the living law for Indonesian people was seen as being rooted not in religious law but rather in customary practices.[183] Moreover, Hurgronje implied that local domestic institutions were the main cause for conflict with how law was implemented.

As with many colonial administrations, the Dutch instituted its own court system with jurisdiction over criminal justice matters. In so doing, the authority of Islamic judges (*qadi*) appointed by the sultan and other local officials began to wane.[184] In Aceh, the struggle for the restoration of Islamic law began with resistance to the Dutch, and later to President Sukarno following independence on August 17, 1945, when Aceh became a part of Indonesia. Sukarno declared that Indonesia was not an Islamic state and would not implement Islamic law,[185] given that the Indonesian archipelago is inhibited by various ethnic, social, religious, and cultural groups, each of which retains its customs and ways of life. Embracing this pluralism, the Republic of Indonesia coined the official motto: *Bhinneka tunggal ika*, or "Unity in diversity."[186]

Moreover in the post-colonial era, several types of laws survived the transition from Dutch colonial rule: (1) laws governing all inhabitants, e.g., the law on industrial property and the law on patents; (2) customary law, which applied to indigenous Indonesians; (3) Islamic laws applicable to all Indonesian Muslims; (4) laws tailored to specific communities in Indonesia, such as the marriage law for Indonesian Christians; and finally (5) the *Burgelijk Wetboek* and the *Wetboek van Koophandel* measures, originally applied to Europeans only, but later extended to cover the Chinese.[187]

Following Indonesia's independence, Aceh was granted provincial status under a military governor. But six years later in 1951, in the effort to streamline administration, Aceh became part of North Sumatra, holding the status of a residency. The people tried to regain provincial status and their aspirations eventually materialized, following a diplomatic mission appointed by the prime minister to solve this issue. The legal basis for the establishment of Aceh was first, Law UU 24/1956 regarding the establishment of Aceh Province; second, a decree by Indonesia's prime minister, No. 1/MISSI/1959, conferring "special territory" status upon the province of Aceh along with a high degree of autonomy with respect to its religion, education, and traditions (*adat*); and, third, Law No. 5/1974 on the "Principles of Regional Government Administration," wherein the status of Aceh as a "Special Region" was confirmed.[188]

It was on September 21, 1953 that Daud Beureueh, the Acehnese leader of DI/TII (Darul Islam/Tentera Islam Indonesia), declared that Aceh should be an Islamic state and should not be subject to Indonesian law or secular law.[189] He incited a rebellion against the Sukarno regime that ended when the Indonesian government sent Col. M. Jassin to persuade him to rejoin Indonesia. Eventually, Daud Beureueh agreed to rejoin but was exiled by the government to Jakarta.[190] As a result, Aceh was given the status of "special territory."

The Acehnese people still feel that they do not constitute a part of Indonesia. The rebellion lead by Daud Beureueh inspired other groups to claim that Aceh does not belong to Indonesia. In 1976 Hasan di Tiro, the president of the Aceh Sumatra National Liberation Front (ANSLF), declared that Aceh should be an independent state. He, however, did not proclaim an Islamic state or the desire to implement Islamic law for Aceh.

Rather, his purpose was to bring classical nationalism to the Acehnese people.[191]

Another factor contributing to popular support for independence has been unhappiness over the unequal distribution of benefits from the large industrial enterprises and plantations along Aceh's east coast. The discovery of substantial reserves of natural gas near Lhokseumawe, Aceh Utara in the early 1970s led to the establishment of large extraction and processing facilities, as well as associated industries.[192] This became one of the reasons for Hasan di Tiro's promotion of "Gerakan Aceh Merdeka" (Free Aceh Movement) or GAM. In 1976 Hasan di Tiro failed to win a tender contract at the P. T. Arun oil fields. As a result, he saw that "the benefits of this factory would not go the Acehnese people."[193] As di Tiro himself wrote in *The Price of Freedom*, this was despite the fact that he had "close business relationships with the top fifty U.S. corporations in the fields of petrochemicals, shipping construction, aviation, manufacturing and food processing industries."[194]

After returning to Aceh at the end of 1976, Hasan emerged at the military camp of Panton Weng, where he stayed from November 1–29, 1976. It was here that he called on selected Acehnese leaders to meet him. "The first order of things," he said, "is to make the Acehnese opinion leaders understand the political process in which our people and our country are involved: we are in the process of being swallowed by the Javanese colonialists and being put to death as a nation, so that the Javanese can inherit our land."[195]

Hasan's stance had major implications for the revival of Acehnese historical consciousness. He gave Acehnese leaders and his followers several books so that they could better understand Acehnese history. GAM viewed the Javanese as the "real enemy" of Aceh, ever since it had been colonized by the Dutch. Soon GAM spread throughout the country, especially on the Sumatra islands. Hasan maintains that the people already knew that the Javanese were their enemy, but no one brought up the matter with the Indonesian Javanese regime, which they all detested. This situation demonstrates the gap between the people of Aceh, Sumatra, and the Indonesian-Javanese regime.[196] Hasan also contends that Javanese Indonesia was an illegally constituted state that had been maintained by using terrorism as a national policy.[197]

In other cases throughout 1989 and 1990, the government and military authorities insisted that the violent disturbances in Aceh were the work of criminal gangs, and that they had no political motivation. Yet, the perpetrators were soon identified as members of the "Security Disturbance Movement" (Gerakan Pengacau Keamanan) or GPK, a government-coined term generally used to describe rebel movements.[198] In recent years the government has also referred to GAM as an "armed civilian gang" (Gerombolan Sipil Bersenjata, GSB).[199] In 2003 the government began labeling GAM a "terrorist group."[200]

While GAM has been in existence since 1976, only since the late 1990s has it developed a significant popular base, a steady source of arms, and a relatively well-organized command structure.[201] The membership of its armed wing, Angkatan Gerakan Aceh Merdeka (AGAM) has been estimated at between fifteen thousand to twenty-seven thousand people, but they have only a few thousand modern firearms.[202] It was reported that "some of GAM's membership was trained in Libya. In 1989, over one hundred Libyan-trained GAM guerillas returned to Aceh with rudimentary military training to try to give the then-moribund rebellion a new lease on life."[203]

To curb this rebellion, President Suharto declared Aceh an area of military operation (Daerah Operasi Militer, DOM). Many Indonesian army personnel were sent to Aceh to fight GAM, both in villages and forests. Through 1989 and the first half of 1990, some six thousand territorial forces normally stationed in the region were mobilized to conduct counter-insurgency operations against the GPK. In July 1990, Suharto ordered the deployment of a further six thousand troops, including two battalions of the Army's Special Forces Command (Komando Pasukan Khusus) or Kopassus, and other elite counterinsurgency units.[204] The number of Indonesian troops increased each year. In 1999 it was reported that police strength was estimated at three thousand. The armed forces numbered some seven to eight thousand troops, including one thousand marines.[205] The outcome of this maneuver was that over a thousand Acehnese people were killed in the first three years of operations. It was reported that 871 were killed outright by the army, and 378 were missing and later turned up dead. More than five hundred others are listed as "disappeared" and have never been found.[206]

The operations ended on August 8, 1998, when General Wiranto, the commander of Indonesia's armed forces, apologized to the Acehnese people on behalf of the government. Indonesia's socio-political situation had serious implications on the conflict of Aceh. This was due, in part, to the government's weakness during the period 1998–1999. Consequently, since 1999 there have been many independence organizations in Aceh concerned with finding solutions to this problem.

One of the government's options for solving the conflict is to give the Acehnese people the right to implement Islamic law. The government has offered several alternatives, both in Banda Aceh, the capital city of Aceh, and Jakarta, on how to go about implementing Islamic law. According to some scholars, this will help solve the political problem,[207] because adherence to Islamic law in Aceh dates back to the first coming of Islam.[208] This was perhaps also the reason behind the government granting special autonomy to Aceh through Law No. 44/1999, allowing it to implement *shariah* precepts in its cultural and educational affairs.[209]

During former President Abdurrahman Wahid's administration, four days before he was impeached, the national parliament passed Law No. 18/2001 conferring special autonomy on the province of Nanggroe Aceh Darussalam (NAD), making it a "Special Region."[210] This law represented an important development in Jakarta's Aceh policy approach, as it sought to convince the Acehnese to remain part of Indonesia by granting them considerable powers of self-governance. The NAD law was formally ratified on August 9, 2001 by President Megawati, who described the legislation as her government's "main pillar for conflict resolution" in Aceh.[211]

The key provisions of the law are the following: a considerably increased revenue sharing of income from natural resources; the use of regional symbols and flags, although not as symbols of sovereignty; direct elections of the governor and vice-governor, and of regents and vice regents; the appointments, but not dismissals, by the central authorities of the provincial police chief and the head of the provincial prosecutor's office, which must be approved by the governor; and finally the establishment of a *shariah* court.[212] The law also stated that the main purpose of implementing *shariah* was to uphold the basic tenet of justice in Islam by delivering social welfare (*maqasid al-Shariah*) to the Acehnese people.[213]

The Dynamics of Implementing Islamic Law in Aceh

The NAD law (Law No. 18/2001) has both its supporters and detractors. Supporters cite several reasons for why the law should be implemented. The first is the fact that Aceh has historically adhered to Islamic law for many years.[214] Accordingly, any other legal system is irrelevant because it is not based on Acehnese tradition and history, which are colored with Islamic teachings. Supporters of the NAD law claim that the Indonesian legal system is not compatible with Acehnese traditions.[215] This is because, from the coming of Islam until Aceh became a province of Indonesia, that particular legal system was never in use.[216]

Supporters of the NAD law argue that implementing Islamic law is one way to resolve the conflict in Aceh. This view is also cited by members of parliament in Jakarta when providing their opinions on the issue. A faction of the Indonesian army fully supports the bill of special autonomy for Aceh, but they propose that legal penalties in Aceh must be based on the Indonesian system of law.[217] The PDI-P (Parti Demokrasi Indonesia Perjuangan), an Indonesian political party, also supports implementing the law, because they believe that solving the conflict in Aceh requires not only a military approach but also a religious one.[218]

The Acehnese elite have not raised any significant criticism with local members of parliament, who were elected in June 1999. The International Crisis Group (ICG) has reported, however, that this group is not particularly representative of Acehnese opinion in general, since many of its members are based in Jakarta rather than in the province.[219] ICG also noted that the poor and less educated majority mistrusted the legislators, particularly the provincial parliament. Moreover, this segment of society knows little about the law's implications for their individual lives.[220]

The law, according to supporters, represents the demands of Acehnese society. Thus, they argue, that ever since Aceh became part of Indonesia, the people could feel that they were no longer Acehnese because they were following the secular law of Indonesia. Consequently, when the government granted the right to implement Islamic law, the Acehnese people felt that they had become "more Acehnese."[221]

Another reason for supporting the law is that it would supposedly eliminate moral decadency in Aceh, in the form of such practices as *korupsi* (corruption), *kolusi* (collution), and *nepotisme* (nepotism), collectively KKN.[222] This view holds that KKN in Aceh is very widespread among local government officials.[223] When I visited offices in Banda Aceh and Lhokseumawe, I noticed that civil servants were keen to initiate large-scale projects. They routinely increase the budget, adding more rupiahs to each project.[224] Some *shariah* proponents feel that Islamic law would eliminate such practices in local government.

Detractors, meanwhile, hold their own arguments for why they are against the NAD law. Any attempt to implement Islamic law in Aceh, they maintain, would represent a step toward formalizing and symbolizing Islamic teachings.[225] These views come from Islamic liberal thinkers in Jakarta, especially from JIL (Jaringan Islam Liberal) and NU (Nahdlatul Ulama) youth.[226] For Azyumardi Azra, there is no state in the Muslim world that could be adopted as a model for the implementation of Islamic law. Consequently, he is very skeptical about the possibility of this movement succeeding in Aceh. Moreover, he refers to the implementation of Islamic law in Aceh as merely a token "gift" from the government for "historical romanticism" purposes.[227]

Implementing Islamic law will not solve the conflict in Aceh, according to those who oppose the NAD law.[228] Rather, they contend that the most important means of settling problems in Aceh is through the empowerment of civil society and improvement in the socio-economic sphere. They further argue that efforts to apply Islamic law have been primarily cosmetic; that is, they are only concerned with symbolic practices,[229] such as the use of Arabic-Malay calligraphy on government offices and streets. Suraiya Kamaruzzaman, a woman activist in Banda Aceh and the founder of Flower Aceh, makes the point that those interpreting Islamic law—the *ulama*, military, and civilian authorities—appear to have focused on the implementation of *shariah* by only emphasizing matters of individual worship such as the *jilbab*, the Friday prayer, and fasting during Ramadan. She contends that Islamic law is not the answer to the war in Aceh.[230]

Another argument made against the NAD law is that its application in Aceh only focuses on provisions relating to women.[231] One of the most controversial issues of implementing Islamic law in Aceh is the stricture demanding women wear the *jilbab* (a long coat or cloak; more generally, any type of outer garment that covers a woman from the shoulders to the ankles). Nurjannah Ismail, a gender activist in Aceh, maintains that while "Islamic law is about handling women's matters," it "does not mean that the men can do anything to women, including enforcing issues of *aurah*."[232] This term refers to the part of a person's body that must be covered when in the presence of anyone but a spouse; for men this is from the navel to the knees, for women from the upper chest to the knees.[233]

This argument regarding the law's focus on women is readily refuted by supporters of the NAD law. For instance, Marlinda Puteh, wife of the Aceh ex-governor, argues that since women hold a high position in Islam as pillars of the state, the first step in promoting Islamic law in Aceh is to have Acehnese women wear the *jilbab* in public to demonstrate that they are true Muslims.[234] In Aceh, Wilayatul Hisbah, the "vice and virtue patrol" or "religious police," carries out many "sweepings," involving women who wear tight clothing instead of the *jilbab*. Al-Yasa Abubakar, who is a scholar and head of the *shariah* division at the State Institute of Islamic Studies in Banda Aceh, argues that these actions do not constitute "sweepings," but are only meant to socialize Islamic law in the city.[235]

Marlinda Puteh also supports these actions because, for her, *shariah* will succeed if women begin to present a good image of Aceh, and this starts with women's dress. [236]

As the debate continues, efforts to implement Islamic law in Aceh have involved a number of legislative steps, including:

- Law No. 44/1999, giving Aceh the right to determine matters relating to religious and cultural affairs, education, and the role of *ulama*
- Law No. 18/2001, granting Aceh special autonomy
- Regional Regulation No. 5/2001, concerning a framework for the application of Islamic law
- Regional Regulation No. 33/2001, delineating the *shariah* organizational structure in Aceh

The local government has also produced a series of *qanun* to serve as the framework for implementing Islamic law in Aceh:

- *Qanun* No. 10/2002 on forming an Islamic court in NAD (Nanggroe Aceh Darussalam)
- *Qanun* No. 11/2002 on the application of *shariah* in *aqidah* (theology), *ibada* (worship), and *syiar* (propagation)
- *Qanun* No. 12/2003 on *khamar* (alcohol)
- *Qanun* No. 13/2003 on *maysir* (gambling)
- *Qanun* No. 14/2003 on *khalwat* (close proximity)

In addition to these various legal instruments, one of the basic steps needed for applying Islamic law in daily life is education. Al-Yasa Abubakar says that Islamic law will not be fully implemented until the Acehnese people become better educated. According to him, the first step is not to promote the law, but to educate the public about what *shariah* is. If people understand the real *shariah*, it will not be necessary to regulate and promote the law because the real goal is aimed at practicing Islamic teaching in a holistic manner (*Islamic kaffah*).[237] That is why the issue of Islamic law in Aceh is not about discussing the *hudud* and so on, but rather, it is about education. This idea is also supported by Yusuf Hasan, an Islamic leader in Banda Aceh, who says that the implementation of *hudud* will take place in the next sixty years, that is, after society becomes better educated and understands *shariah*.[238]

After NAD law was passed, GAM demonstrated its rejection of special autonomy for Aceh by increasing its attacks on state facilities. The conflict led many Acehnese government officials at the village and district levels in GAM-controlled areas to either abandon their offices or to reach some sort of arrangement with GAM members.[239] GAM's founding father, Hasan di Tiro, dismissed Jakarta's plans to introduce Islamic law as "irrelevant" because "the struggle of the Acehnese people never had anything to do with *shari'ah*."[240]

CONCLUSION

In exploring the implementation of Islamic law in Kelantan and Aceh, we can see both similarities and differences. The first point of similarity is that the Kelantan state and Aceh Province had adhered to Islamic law since the coming of Islam, and Islamic law was applied in both regions through their respective Islamic kingdoms and the role of *ulama*. Traditional Islamic education played an important role in disseminating Islamic law to the people. In Kelantan, the traditional institution was known as the *pondok*, while in Aceh, it is referred to as *dayah*.

Similarly, Islamic law in Kelantan and Aceh was eliminated first by colonialists and later by national governments. Up until today, neither Malaysia nor Indonesia has become an Islamic state. In Indonesia, the state is based on Pancasila (Five Pillars).[241] In both Kelantan and Aceh, I would argue that the struggle to implement Islamic law actually involves efforts to implement *hudud* (penal) law. This is a misinterpretation of Islamic law. As was discussed early on, Islamic law is the entire corpus of legal reasoning (*ijtihad*), it represents not just *shariah*, the "sacred law of Islam," but embodies human interpretation, modification, and application, as required to meet the needs of modern society.

The implementation of Islamic law in Kelantan and Aceh became a political issue for the elite in both Malaysia and Indonesia. The government's response to the issue in Malaysia was quite different from that of Indonesia. But, I believe that in both cases the issue has become more political than religious. For PAS, as the administrator of Kelantan, the issue of implementing Islamic law was adopted as a strategy to attract votes. In Indonesia, the political elite made the issue of Islamic law in Aceh a strategy to resolve conflict, as well as to win national and local elections in Aceh.[242]

Another similarity is that so-called Islamic law in both Kelantan and Aceh is *hudud* law. But this law has not yet been fully implemented in either place. Although, some rules have, in fact, been passed based on Islamic teachings for the community, such as the "sweepings" or *razia* by police in the streets and public areas, such as cafes. The government in Kelantan introduced many measures related to Islamic teachings in public areas, but those are still primarily symbolic. The same is true of Aceh, where the government has attempted to promote the Arabic script, especially for office logos. It is safe to say that the provincial government and its emphasis on religious symbols—such as the Islamic dress code and the usage of Arabic signs and letterheads, as well as public lashings for petty offences like the sale and consumption of food during Ramadan—are creating an image of *shariah* based more on violence than on social justice.[243]

With regard to the differences involved in attempting to apply Islamic law, political means were used in Kelantan through the introduction of the Hudud Bill after PAS won the 1990 election. By contrast, in Aceh the issues surrounding the application of Islamic law are much more complex. While the Islamic law movement began after independence when Acehnese leaders declared Aceh to be an Islamic state, the issue of Islamic law became a means of solving problems in the Aceh conflict. Here, the government realized that the implementation of Islamic law was bound up with the granting of special autonomy to Aceh.

Another difference is that, in Kelantan, the method used to implement Islamic law has been through peaceful means, unlike the violence experienced in Aceh. And while the conflict in Kelantan is still alive in the political arena, it does not have the serious implications for the people that it does for its neighbors. In Aceh, GAM (the Aceh Liberation Movement) rejected special autonomy as well as the right to implement Islamic law, and instead has used arms in its efforts to establish an independent state. In response, the TNI (Indonesian National Military) comes to Aceh under the umbrella of Indonesian secular law.[244]

The difference is the implementation of Islamic law in Kelantan has been a PAS strategy to gain votes and to pressure the government's party (UMNO) on the issue of Islamic law and statehood. For these reasons it is easy to understand why the government does not support PAS's demands to implement Islamic law in Kelantan. In Aceh, however, the issue of

Islamic law is seen by the central government as a means of resolving conflict as well as gaining political support. There has been a serious effort on the part of the Indonesian government to help the local government implement Islamic law.

Finally, in Kelantan non-Muslims have challenged the implementation of Islamic law by opposing PAS's demands. Even though the Hudud Bill applies only to Muslims, non-Muslims see that it could have an impact on other religions. For instance, the real opposition to efforts to spread Buddhism among Malaysians tends mostly to come from the Majlis Agama Islam (Muslim Religious Council), which supervises the administration of Islam and looks after the interest of the Muslim population in the state.[245] In Aceh, non-Muslims supported the need for implementation of Islamic law, saying that they understood that Acehnese society had implemented Islamic law for hundreds of years.[246] But they urged that Islamic law apply only to Muslims.[247]

In summary, the dynamic nature of the interpretation of Islamic law in two of Southeast Asia's Muslim countries has created very different, yet similar, situations. Malaysia and Indonesia have not been able to apply Islamic law successfully because of the many challenges they have faced, both external and internal. At the same time, responses to the modern era from segments of each of their populations include a rejection of the secular law promulgated by their national governments. This study has shown that implementing Islamic law is not a good method for resolving conflict. In other words, there is no need to establish Islamic law formally through the political process, because when politics enters the religious arena it carries with it many interests.

NOTES

1   J. N. D. Anderson, *Islamic Law in the Modern World* (New York: New York University Press, 1959), 83.

2   Nobuyuki Yasuda, "Law and Development in ASEAN Countries," *ASEAN Economic Bulletin* 10, no. 2 (1993): 144–54. See also Christine Dobbin, "Islamic Revivalism in Minangkabau at the Turn of the Nineteenth Century," *Modern Asian Studies* 8, no. 3 (1974), 319–45; Taufik Abdullah, "*Adat* and Islam: An Examination of Conflict in Minangkabau," *Indonesia* 2 (1966): 1–24; Idem., "Some Notes on the Kaba Tjindua Mato: An Example of Minangkabau Traditional Literature," *Indonesia* 9 (1970), 1–22.

3   On the coming of Islam to Malay, see G. W. J. Drewes, "New Light on the Coming of Islam to Indonesia," in *Readings on Islam in Southeast Asia*, eds. Ahmad Ibrahim, et al. (Singapore: Institute of Southeast Asian Studies, 1985), 7–19.

4   M. B. Hooker, *Islamic Law in South-east Asia* (Singapore: Oxford University Press, 1984).

5   Nobuyuki Yasuda, "Law and Development," 148. See also, Abdullah Alwi Haji Hassan, *The Administration of Islamic Law in Kelantan* (Kuala Lumpur: Dewan Bahasa dan Pustaka, 1996), xli–lii.

6   For a brief discussion of this movement, see Holk H. Dengel, *Darul Islam dan Kartosuwirjo* [The Islamic State and Kartosuwirjo] (Jakarta: Sihar Harapan, 1995).

7   Fred R. von der Mehden, "Malaysia: Islam and Multiethnic Polities," in *Islam in Asia: Religion, Politics, and Society*, ed. John L. Esposito (New York: Oxford University Press, 1987), 187; G. W. Choudhury, *Islam and the Modern Muslim World* (Kuala Lumpur: WHS Publications, 1993), 163–64. See also Joseph M. Fernando, "The Position of Islam in the Constitution of Malaysia," *Journal of Southeast Asian Studies* 37, no. 2 (2006): 249–66; Herbert Feith and Lance Castles, eds., *Pemikiran Politik Indonesia 1945–1965* [Indonesian Political Thinking, 1945–1965], trans. Min Yubahar (Jakarta: LP3ES, 1988), 208.

8   For Daud's statement, see Feith and Castles, *Pemikiran Politik Indonesia*, 208–11.

9   However, it is well documented that PAS also uses radical strategies. See, e.g., Farish A. Noor, "Blood, Sweat and Jihad: The Radicalization of the Political Discourse of the Pan-Malaysian Islamic Party (PAS) from 1982 Onwards," *Contemporary Southeast Asia* 25, no. 2 (2003): 200–32; Idem., "The Localization of Islamist Discourse in the Tafsîr of Tuan Guru Nik Aziz Nik Mat, Murshid'ul

Am of PAS," in *Malaysia Islam, Society and Politics*, eds. Virginia Hooker and Norani Othmad (Singapore: ISEAS, 2003), 195–235; Idem., "Reaping the Bitter Harvest After Twenty Years of State Islamization: The Malaysian Experience Post-September 11," in *Terrorism in the Asia Pacific: Threat and Response*, ed. Rohan Gunaratna (Singapore: Eastern University Press, 2003). For details on the history of PAS, see Farish A. Noor, *Islam Embedded: The Historical Development of the Pan-Malaysian Islamic Party PAS, 1951–2003* (Kuala Lumpur: Malaysian Sociological Research Institute, 2004).

10 See Shukri Ahmad, "Implikasi Pengaruh Ulama Terhadap Halatuju Perubahan Pemikiran Politik Masyarakat Islam Wilayah Utara Semenanjung Malaysia Dari 1950-an Hingga 1990-an" [The Implications of *Ulama*'s Influence in a Changing Society's Political Thought in North Malaysia from 1950 to 1990], *Journal of Ushuluddin* 14 (2001): 99.

11 International Crisis Group, "Aceh: Can Autonomy Stem the Conflict?" Asia Briefing No. 18, June 27, 2001.

12 For a chronology of Aceh's legal status, see Kaoy Syah and Lukman Hakiem, eds., *Keistimewaan Aceh dalam Lintasan Sejarah: Proses Pembentukan UU No.44/1999* [The Special Case of Aceh in History: The Process of Forming Law No. 44/1999] (Jakarta: Pengurus Besar Al-Jami'iyatul Washliyyah, 2000).

13 For a brief discussion of this issue, see Kamaruzzaman Bustamam-Ahmad, *Satu Dasawarwa the Clash of Civilizations* [The Tenth Year of the Clash of Civilizations] (Yogyakarta: Ar-Ruzz, 2003) 195–203; Idem., "Menakar Harga Kemarahan Orang Aceh: Etnograpi Kekerasan di Indonesia," [The Cost of Acehnese Anger: The Ethnography of Violence in Indonesia] in *Tamaddun dan Sejarah: Etnografi Kekerasan di Aceh* [Civilization and History: The Ethnography of Violence in Aceh], ed. Hasanuddin Yusuf Adan (Yogyakarta: Prismasophie Press, 2003), 9–38.

14 Muhammad Alfian Dja'far, "Independensi Mahkamah Syariah Nanggroew Aceh Darussalam" [The Islamic Courts' Independence in Nanggroe Aceh Darussalam] (bachelor's thesis, State Institute of Islamic Studies, Yogyakarta, 2003).

15 For a good analysis of this topic, see C. Van Dijk, "Is God a Gangster? Political and Religious Authority and Religious Sentiments" (paper presented at IIAS and ISIM Workshop on "Fatwas and the Dissemination of Religious Authority in Indonesia," Leiden, October 31, 2002), 1–10.

16 For accounts of this controversial debate, see Rosli Ibrahim, "Isu Malaysia Negara Islam: Antara Kenyataan dan Kejahila" [The Malaysian Issue of the Islamic State: Between Reality and Stupidity], *Siasah Bil.* 7, November 29–30, 2001; Tengku Ahmad Muhammad, "Dikir Barat Kelantan dan Kriteria: Perlukah Reformasi di Dunia Hiburan?" in *Seumbi* (Pulau Pinang: Planet Hijau Media, 2001), 34–35;

Saifulizam Mohamad, "Antara Hudud Allah dan 'Hudud PAS'" [Between the Penal Law of God and the Penal Law of PAS], *MASSA News* (July 13–19, 2002), 16–17.

17   See Ann Elizabeth Mayer, ed., *Property, Social Structure and Law in the Modern Middle East* (Albany: State University of New York Press, 1985); Idem., "Religious Legitimacy and Constitutionalism: The Saudi Basic Law and the Moroccan Constitution Compared," in *Religion and Law in the Global Village*, eds. David E. Guinn, et al. (Atlanta: Scholars Press, 1999), 81–97; Abdullahi Ahmed An-Na'im, *Toward an Islamic Reformation: Civil Liberties, Human Rights, and International Law* (Syracuse: Syracuse University Press, 1990).

18   See, e.g., Hooker, *Islamic Law*; Idem., ed., *Islam in South-East Asia* (Leiden: E. J. Brill, 1983); Idem., "The State and Shariah in Indonesia, 1945–1995" in *Indonesia: Law and Society*, ed. Tim Lindsey (Sydney: Federation Press, 1999); "Introduction: Islamic Law in South-east Asia," *Australian Journal of Asian Law* 4, no. 3 (2002): 213—31; Idem., *Islam Mazhab Indonesia: Fatwa-Fatwa dan Perubahan Sosial* (Bandung: Teraju Mizan, 2003).

19   See, e.g., Muhammad Atho Mudzhar, *Fatwa-Fatwa Majelis Ulama Indonesia* (Jakarta: INIS, 1993); Idem., "The Council of Indonesian Ulama' on Muslims' Attendance at Christmas Celebrations," in *Islamic Legal Interpretations*, eds. Muhammad Khalid Masud, Brinkley Messick, and David S. Power (Cambridge, MA: Harvard University Press, 1996), 230–41; Idem., "The Ulama', the Government, and Society in Modern Indonesia: The Indonesian Council of Ulama' Revisited," in *Islam in the Era of Globalization: Muslim Attitudes Towards Modernity and Identity*, ed. Johan Meuleuman (Jakarta: INIS, 2001), 315–26.

20   See, e.g., Kamaruzzaman Bustamam-Ahmad, "Relasi Ugama [Islam] dan Politik" [The Relationship Between Religion and Politics], *Siasah*, October 26–29, 2001; Idem., "Perdebatan Mengenai Negara Islam" [Debate on the Islamic State], *Siasah*, November 26–27, 2001. See also Idem., "Hubungan Agama dan Negara" [The Relationship between Religion and State], *Pemikir* 30 (2002): 93–119; Idem., "Konsep Negara Era Moden" [The Concept of State in the Modern Era], *Pemikir* 31 (2003): 233–58. *Pemikir* is the top journal among Malaysian scholars. It is published as a collaborative effort between Utusan Melayu, Institut Kajian Strategik dan Antarbangsa (ISIS), and the journal *Foreign Affairs*.

21   See Kamaruzzaman Bustamam-Ahmad, *Islam Historis: Dinamika Studi Islam di Indonesia* [Islamic History: The Dynamics of Islamic Studies in Indonesia] (Yogyakarta: Galang Press, 2002).

22   See, e.g., Khairuddin Nasution, *Status Wanita di Asia Tenggara: Studi Terhadap Perundang-Undangan Perkawinan Muslim Kontemporer di Indonesia dan Malaysia* [The Status of Women in Southeast Asia: A Study of Muslim Contemporary Marriage Law in Indonesia and Malaysia] (Jakarta: INIS, 2002).

23   See, e.g., John R. Bowen, "'You May Not Give it Away': How Social Norms Shape Islamic Law in Contemporary Indonesian Jurisprudence," *Islamic Law and Society* 5, no. 3 (1998): 382–408.

24   See, e.g., Nico Kaptein, *The Muhimmât al-Nafâ'is: A Bilingual Meccan Fatwa Collection for Indonesian Muslims from the End of the Nineteenth Century* (Jakarta: INIS, 1997); Mudzhar, *Fatwa-Fatwa*; Idem., "The Council of Indonesian *Ulama*," 230–41; Idem., "The *Ulama*," the Government, and Society," 315–26; Nurhadi, "Muslims' Participation in Christmas Celebrations: A Critical Study on the Fatwa of the Council of Indonesian Ulama," *Al-Jamiah* 40, no. 2 (2002): 280–301.

25   Rifyal Ka'bah, "Pluralisme dalam Perspektif Syariah" [Pluralism in *Shariah* Perspective], *Mimbar Hukum* 5 (2001): 7–14.

26   Masdar F. Mas'udi, "Hak Azasi Manusia dalam Islam" [Human Rights in Islam], in *Diseminasi Hak Asasi Manusia: Perspektif dan Aksi* [The Dissemination of Human Rights: Perspectives and Action], eds. E. Shobirin Nadj and Naning Mardiniah (Jakarta: LP3ES, 2000) 63–72.

27   Akh. Minhaji, "Problem Gender dalam Perspektif Sejarah Hukum Islam" [Gender Problems from the Perspective of the History of Islamic Law], *Nabila* 1 (1998): 14–26.

28   Akh. Minhaji, "Zakat dalam Konteks Otonomi Daerah," in *Tafsir Baru Studi Islam dalam Era Multi Kultural* [New Interpretations of Islamic Studies in a Multicultural Era], ed. M. Amin Abdullah (Yogyakarta: IAIN Sunan Kalijaga-Kurnia Kalam Semesta, 2002), 211–36

29   Akh. Minhaji, "Supremasi Hukum dalam Masyarakat Madani: Perspektif Sejarah Hukum Islam," *Unisia* 41 (2000): 23–33.

30   See, e.g., Amiq, "Two Fatwas on Jihad against the Dutch Colonization in Indonesia: A Prosopographical Approach to the Study of Fatwa," *Studia Islamika* 5, no. 3 (1998): 77–124; Nico Kaptein, "Acceptance, Approval and Aggression: Some Fatwas Concerning the Colonial Administration in the Dutch East Indies," *Al-Jamiah*, 38, no. 2 (2000): 297–309.

31   See, e.g., Syamsul Anwar, "Islamic Jurisprudence of Christian-Muslim Relations: Toward A Reinterpretation," *Al-Jamiah* 61 (1997): 128–53; Tim Penulis Paramadina, *Fiqh Lintas Agama: Membangun Masyarakat Inklusif-Pluralis* (Jakarata: Paramadina and The Asia Foundation, 2003).

32   Abdullah Alwi Haji Hassan, *Administration of Islamic Law.*

33   Mehrun Siraj, "Women and the Law: Significant Developments in Malaysia," *Law and Society Review* 28, no. 3 (1994): 561–72, cited in Khoiruddin Nasution, *Status Wanita di Asia Tenggara*, 25–26.

34   Marzuki Wahid and Nurrohman, "Dimensi Fundamentalisme dalam Politik Formalisasi Syariat Islam: Kasus Nanggroe Aceh Darussalam, [The Fundamentalism Dimension in the Political Formalization of *Shariah* Islam: The Case of Nanggroe Aceh Darussalam], *Tashwirul Afkar* 13 (2002): 34–57.

35   See, e.g., Mahmoud Ayyub, "Sulit, Menerapkan Sistem Politik Berbasis Syariah," [Difficult to Apply Political System Based on *Shariah*] *Tashwirul Afkar* 13 (2002): 121–25.

36   See Mark R. Woodward, *Toward a New Paradigm: Recent Developments in Indonesian Islamic Thought* (Tempe: Center for Southeast Asian Studies, Arizona State University, 1996).

37   John Strawson, "Encountering Islamic Law," *Mimbar Studi* 3 (1999): 215.

38   M. Atho Mudzhar, "Social History Approach to Islamic Law," *Al Jamiah* 61 (1998): 79.

39   Ibid.

40   See my exploration in "Kontribusi Daerah Aceh Terhadap Perkembangan Awal Hukum Islam di Indonesia" [Aceh's Contribution to the Early Development of Islamic Law in Indonesia], *Al-Jamiah: Journal of Islamic Studies* 64 (1999): 146–50.

41   See, e.g., M. Atho Mudzhar, "Studi Hukum Islam dengan Pendekatan Sosiologi" [The Study of Islam from a Sociological Perspective], in *Antologi Studi Islam: Teori and Practice* [Anthology of Islamic Studies: Theory and Practice], ed. M. Amin Abdullah, et al. (Yogyakarta: IAIN Sunan Kalijaga, 2000), 239–71.

42   On *ummah* see Maysam J. Al Faruqi, "*Umma*: The Orientalist and The Qur'anic Concept of Identity," *Journal of Islamic Studies* (Oxford) 16, no. 1 (2005): 1–34.

43   See, e.g., Lee Kam Hing, 1995, *The Sultanate of Aceh: Relations with the British 1760–1824* (Kuala Lumpur: Oxford University Press, 1995).

44   See generally, Joseph Schacht, *The Origins of Muhammadan Jurisprudence* (Oxford: Claredon Press, 1975); Wael B. Hallaq, *A History of Islamic Legal Theories: An Introduction to Sunni Usul Fiqh* (Cambridge: Cambridge University Press, 1997); Robert Gleave, *Inevitable Doubt: Two Theories of Shi'i Jurisprudence* (Leiden: E. J. Brill, 2000); R. Gleave and E. Kermeli, eds., *Islamic Law: Theory and Practice* (New York: I. B. Tauris, 1997); Bernard G. Weiss, ed., *Studies in Islamic Legal Theory* (Leiden: E. J. Brill, 2002); Baber Johansen, *Contingency in a Sacred Law: Legal and Ethical Norms in the Muslim Fiqh* (Leiden: E. J. Brill, 1999); Mohd. Khalid Masud, et al., eds., *Islamic Legal Interpretation* (Harvard: Harvard University Press, 1996); David S. Powers, *Studies in Qur'an and Hadith: The Formation of the Islamic Law of Inheritance* (Berkeley: University of California Press, 1986);

Mayer, *Property, Social Structure and Law*; Idem., *Islam and Human Rights: Tradition and Politics* (Boulder, CO: Westview Press, 1991); An-Naim, *Toward an Islamic Reformation*; Mahmud Saedon Awang Othman, "Islamic Law and Its Codification," *IIU Law Journal* 1, no. 1 (1989): 51–82; Robert Roberts, *The Social Laws of the Qur'an* (London: Curzon Press, 1924); Tahir Mahmood, ed., *Human Rights in Islamic Law* (New Delhi: Genuine Publications, 1993); David E. Guinn, et al., eds., *Religion and Law in the Global Village* (Atlanta: Scholars Press, 1999).

45   A. Qodri Azizy, "Juristic Differences (*Ikhtilaf*) in Islamic Law: Its Meaning, Early Discussions, and Reasons (A Lesson for Contemporary Characteristics)," *Al Jamiah* 39, no. 2 (2001): 264.

46   On Joseph Schacht, see George F. Hourani, "Joseph Schacht, 1902–69," *Journal of the American Oriental Society* 90, no. 2 (1970), 163–67; Aharon Layish, "Notes on Joseph Schacht's Contribution to the Study of Islamic Law," *British Journal of Middle Eastern Studies* 9, no. 2 (1982), 132–40; Akh. Minhaji, *Kontroversi Pembentukan Hukum Islam: Kontribusi Joseph Schacht* (Yogyakarta: UII Press, 2001); Faisar Ananda Arfa, *Sejarah Pembentukan Hukum Islam: Studi Kritis tentang Hukum Islam di Barat* (Jakarta: Pustaka Firdaus, 1996).

47   Joseph Schacht, *An Introduction to Islamic Law* (Oxford: Clarendon Press, 1964), 1.

48   Zafar Ishaq Ansari, "Foreword," in *Theories of Islamic Law: The Methodology of Ijtihad*, ed. Imran Ahsan Khan Nyazee (Islamabad: International Islamic University of Islamabad, Islamic Research Institute and International Institute of Islamic Thought [IIIT], 1994), v.

49   Akh. Minhaji, "A Problem of Methodological Approaches to Islamic Law Studies," *Al-Jamiah* 63 (1999): iv.

50   Akh. Minhaji, *Ahmad Hassan and Islamic Legal Reform in Indonesia (1887– 1958)* (Yogyakarta: Kurnia Kalam Semesta Press, 2001), 20–21; Idem., "Reorientasi Kajian Ushul Fiqh" [Reorientation of Ushul Fiqh], *Al-Jamiah* 62 (1999): 23–24.

51   Mashood A. Baderin, *International Human Rights and Islamic Law* (Oxford: Oxford University Press, 2003), 33.

52   Abdul Azis Dahlan, et al., eds., *Ensiklopedi Hukum Islam*, 1st ed. (Jakarta: Ichtiar Baru van Hoeve, 1997), 333; Kamaruzzaman Bustamam-Ahmad, *Islam Historis*, 224.

53   See, A. Qodri Azizy, *Ekletisme Hukum Nasional: Kompetisi Antara Hukum Islam dan Hukum Umum* (Yogyakarta: Gama Media, 2002), 2–4.

54   Nyazee, *Theories of Islamic Law*, 20–21; Ahmad Hassan, *Pintu Ijtihad Sebelum Tertutup*, trans. Agah Garnadi (Bandung: Pustaka, 1994), 5.

55   Imran Ahsan Khan Nyazee, *Theories of Islamic Law*, 21

56   Ahmad Hassan, *Pintu Ijtihad Sebelum Tertutup*, 4–5.

57   Imran Ahsan Khan Nyazee, *Theories of Islamic Law*, iv.

58   Dahlan, *Ensiklopedi Hukum Islam*, 333. For details about Abu Hanifah, see Ahmad Syurbashi, *Al-Aimmah al-Arba'ah* (Beirut: Dar al-Jil, n.d.), 14–68.

59   On Mu'tazilah, see George F. Hourani, "Islamic and Non-Islamic Origins of Mu'tazilite Ethical Rationalism," *International Journal of Middle East Studies* 7, no. 1 (1976): 59–87.

60   Abdul Wahhab Khallaf, *'Ilm Ushul al-Fiqh* (Beirut: Dar al-Qalam, 1978), 11. This may be translated into English as "the knowledge of *shar'i ahkâm* (legal rules) pertaining to conduct that has been derived from specific evidence."

61   Ibid., 12.

62   Abu Ishaq al-Syirazi, *al-Luma fi Ushul al-Fiqh* (Cairo: Muhammad Ali Sabih, 1900), 4, cited in A. Qodri Azizy, *Ekletisme Hukum Nasional*, 13.

63   Akh Minhaji, *Ahmad Hassan*, 94.

64   Dahlan, *Ensiklopedi Hukum Islam*, 335.

65   Ibid. For the Sunnah, see Muhammad Abdul Rauf, "Al-Hadith: Its Authority and Authenticity," *IIU Law Journal* 1, no. 1 (1989): 1–50.

66   Schacht, *Introduction to Islamic Law*, 1.

67   For further discussion, see Kamaruzzaman Bustamam-Ahmad, "Kontribusi Daerah Aceh," 148.

68   M. Atho Mudzhar, "Social History Approach to Islamic Law," *Al-Jamiah* 61 (1998): 80; Idem., "Dirâsat al-Ahkâm al-Islâmiyyah bin Mandhûr 'Ilm al-Ijtimâ,'" *Al-Jamiah* 65 (2000): 177.

69   Akh Minhaji, *Ahmad Hassan*, 13–15; Idem., "Modern Trends in Islamic Law: Notes on J. N. D. Anderson's Life and Thought," *Al-Jamiah* 39, no. 1 (2001): 8–9.

70   On the formative era, see generally, Hallaq, *History of Islamic Legal Theories*, 1–35.

71   On this issue, see Wael B. Hallaq, "Was the Gate of Ijtihad Closed?" *International Journal of Middle East Studies* 16 (1984): 3–41; Idem., "On the Origins of the Controversy about the Existence of Mujtahids and the Gate of Ijtihad," *Studia Islamica* 63 (1986): 129–41.

72   See generally, Robert W. Hefner, *Civil Islam: Muslim and Democratization in Indonesia* (Oxford: Princeton University Press, 2000), 3–7.

73   See Bassam Tibi, *Islam and the Cultural Accommodation of Social Change*, trans. Clare Krojzl (Boulder, CO: Westview Press, 1991), 64–65; R. Stephen

Humphreys, *Islamic History: A Framework for Inquiry* (Princeton: Princeton University Press, 1991), 210–12.

74   Minhaji, *Modern Trends in Islamic Law*, 13.

75   M. Atho Mudzhar, *Membaca Gelombang Ijtihad: Antara Tradisi dan Liberasi* (Yogyakarta: Titian Ilahi Press, 1998), 177.

76   Minhaji, *Modern Trends in Islamic Law*, 13–17. See also Anderson, *Islamic Law in the Modern World*.

77   Alexander Hamilton, *A New Account of the East Indies, Being the Observations and Remarks of Capt. Alexander Hamilton Who Spent His Time There* (Edinburgh: John Mofman, 1727).

78   Khoo Kay Kim, 1992, "Introduction," in *An Expedition to Trengganu and Kelantan 1895*, ed. Hugh Clifford (Kuala Lumpur: MBRAS, 1992), xi.

79   Abdullah Alwi Haji Hassan, *Administration of Islamic Law*, 1. See also, S. Q. Fatimi, *Islam Comes to Malaysia* (Singapore: Malaysia Sociological Research Institute Ltd., 1963).

80   Mohd. Taib Osman, "Islamization of the Malays: A Transformation of Culture," in *Readings of Islam in Southeast Asia*, eds. Ahmad Ibrahim, et al. (Singapore: ISEAS, 1985), 46.

81   Abdullah Alwi Haji Hassan, *Administration of Islamic Law*, 3.

82   Ibid., 30.

83   Wan Arfah Hamzah and Ramy Bulan, *An Introduction to the Malaysian Legal System* (Selangor: Fajar Bakti, 2003), 109.

84   Abdullah Alwi Haji Hassan, *Administration of Islamic Law*, 69.

85   Ibid., 73.

86   Tengku Razaleigh Hamzah, "The Semangat 46 View," in *Hudud in Malaysia: The Issues at Stake*, edited by Rose Ismail (Selangor: Ilmiah Publishers, 2002), 57.

87   Abdullah Alwi Haji Hassan, *Administration of Islamic Law*, 41–42.

88   The *pondok* in Kelantan, *dayah* in Aceh, and *pesantren* in Java are Islamic boarding schools. Although they have different names, the system is similar. See generally, Abdurrahman Masud, "Why the Pesantren in Indonesia Remains Unique and Stronger," in *Islamic Studies in ASEAN: Presentations of an International Seminar*, eds. Isma-ae Alee, et al. (Pattani: Prince of Songkla University, 2000), 191–202; Zamahksyari Dhofier, *Tradisi Pesantren: Studi tentang Pandangan Hidup Kyai* [The Pesantren Tradition: A Study of the Life View of Kyai] (Jakarta: LP3ES, 1982); M. Dawam Rahardjo, "The Kyai, the Pesantren, and the Village: A Preliminary Sketch," in *Readings on Islam in Southeast Asia*, ed. Ahmad Ibrahim,

et al. (Singapore: Institute of Southeast Asian Studies, 1985), 240–46; Azyumardi Azra, *Pendidikan Islam: Tradisi dan Modernisasi Menuju Milenium Baru* (Jakarta: Logos, 1999), 85–158; Yusny Saby, "Islam and Social Change: The Role of the Ulama in Acehnese Society" (PhD diss., Temple University, 1995), 110–29.

89   Abdullah Alwi Haji Hassan, *Administration of Islamic Law*, 220.

90   Mohd. Redzuan Othman, "Masjid Al-Haram dan Peranannya Dalam Perkembangan Awal Pendidikan dan Intelektualisme Masyarakat Melayu," *Jurnal Usuluddin* 13 (2001): 69–76.

91   Ibid., 71; Amran Kasimin, *Religion and Social Change Among the Indigenous People of the Malay Peninsula* (Kuala Lumpur: Dewan Bahasa dan Pustaka Kementerian Pendidikan Malaysia, 1991), 175.

82   Abdullah Alwi Haji Hassan, *Administration of Islamic Law*, 220.

93   On *madrasa*, see Richard T. Mortel, "Madrasas in Mecca during the Medieval Period: A Descriptive Study Based on Literary Sources," *Bulletin of the School of Oriental and African Studies* 60, no. 2 (1997), 236–52; Olivia Remie Constable, "Reconsidering the Origin of the Funduq," *Studia Islamica* 92 (2001): 195–96.

94   Abdullah Alwi Haji Hassan, *Administration of Islamic Law*, 226–27.

95   Such *madrasa* included, for example, Lorong Tok Semian in Kota Bahru (1910), then the town of Pasir Mas; Madrasah Ibrahimiyyah and Madrasah As-Saniyah Lil-Banat in Pasir Puteh; Madrasah An-Na'im lil Banat in Langgar; Madrasah 'Alawiyyah in Kampong Sireh; Madrasah al-Islah in Kota Bahru; Madrasah Ad-Diniyyah in Gual Periok; Madrasah Yakqubiah in Nipah; Madrasah Arabiyyah in Pengkalan Cengal; Madrasah Sa'adatul Qura in Kemubu; and Madrasah Ad-Diniyyah in Pasir Tekan. See Abdullah Alwi Haji Hassan, *Administration of Islamic Law*, 239.

96   Joseph Liow, "Deconstructing Political Islam in Malaysia: UMNO's Responses to PAS' Religio-Political Dialectic," Working Paper, No. 45 (Singapore: Institute of Defence and Strategic Studies, 2003), ii.

97   See generally, Mohd. Redzuan Othman, "The Middle East Influence on the Development of Religious and Political Thought in Malay Society, 1880–1940" (PhD diss., University of Edinburgh, 1994).

98   Shukri Ahmad, "Implikasi Pengaruh Ulama Terhadap Halatuju Perubahan Pemikiran Politik Masyarakat Islam Wilayah Utara Semenanjung Malaysia Dari 1950an Hingga 1990an," *Jurnal Usuluddin* 14 (2002): 99.

99   "Political Islam in Southeast Asia," Conference Report, School of Advanced International Studies (SAIS), John Hopkins University, March 25, 2003, http://www.sais-jhu.edu/programs/asia/ asiaoverview/Publications/Southeast%20Asia/Political%20Islam%20Report.pdf (accessed October 2004).

100 Jan Stark, "The Islamic Debate in Malaysia: The Unfinished Project," *South East Asia Research* 11, no. 2 (2003): 176–77.

101 Jan Stark, "Constructing an Islamic Model in Two Malaysian States: PAS Rule in Kelantan and Terengganu," *SOJOURN* 19, no. 1 (2004): 52.

102 Liow, *Deconstructing Political Islam*, 2.

103 Norhamshimad Mohd. Yasin, *Islamisation/Malayanisation: A Study on the Role of Islamic Law in Economics Development in Malaysia, 1969–1993* (Kuala Lumpur: Pustaka Hayati, 1996), 191.

104 Jan Stark, "The Islamic Debate in Malaysia: The Unfinished Project," *South East Asia Research* 11, no. 2 (2003): 179.

105 Liow, *Deconstructing Political Islam*, 8.

106 Interview with Datuk Wan Wahid, July 2004.

107 This idea came out of the Malay Conference at Putri Pan Pacific Hotel, Johor, October 11–12, 2004.

108 See also, William Case, *Politics in Southeast Asia: Democracy or Less* (London: Curzon Press, 2002), 137–43.

109 Interview with Zainah Anwar, June 2004.

110 "Mahathir: Malaysia is a 'fundamentalist state,'" CNN.com/World, June 18, 2002, http://archives.cnn.com/2002/WORLD/asiapcf/southeast/06/18/malaysia. mahathir (accessed October 15, 2004).

111 See "Islamic State Document" (ISD), prepared by PAS, November 12, 2003, http://www.parti-pas.org/IslamicStateDocument.php (accessed October 14, 2004).

112 See *Surah al-Maidah* (5:49–50).

113 See *Surah al-Ahzab* (33:36).

114 "The PAS View," in Ismail, *Hudud in Malaysia*, 51–53.

115 Stark, *Constructing an Islamic Model*, 51.

116 See Dahlan, *Ensiklopedi Hukum Islam*, vol. 3: 806–11, vol. 5: 1771–76.

117 Mahathir Mohamad, "Islam Guarantees Justice for All Citizens," in Ismail, *Hudud in Malaysia*, 65.

118 Ibid., 70.

119 "Dr. Mahathir to Aziz: try *hudud* laws now," *New Straits Times*, April 17, 1992.

120 Mohamad, "Islam Guarantees Justice," 73–74. See also, Saifullizam Mohammad, "Antara Hudud Allah dan 'Hudud PAS,'" [Between the Penal Law of God and the

Penal Law of PAS] *MASSA* (Malaysia South-South Association), nos. 13–19, July 16–17, 2002.

121 "DAP opposes *hudud* laws," *New Straits Times*, April 10, 1992.

122 These parties included Parti Keadilan Nasional and Parti Rakyat Malaysia.

123 Mohn Izani bin Mohd. Zain, "Barisan Alternatif Selepas Tiga Tahun," *Minda*, June 2002, 62; Ann Wan Seng, "Kenapa DAP Keluar Barisan Alternatif?" *Siasah*, November 2001, 32–33.

124 Mohd. Hashim Kamali, *Punishment in Islamic Law: An Enquiry into the Hudud Bill of Kelantan* (Kuala Lumpur: Ilmiah Publishers, 2000), 11

125 Ibid., 123.

126 Sisters in Islam, "Letter to the Prime Minister," in Ismail, *Hudud in Malaysia*, 7.

127 Kamali, *Punishment in Islamic Law*, 23.

128 See Salbiah Ahmad, "*Zina* and Rape under the Syariah Criminal Code (II) Bill 1993 (Kelantan)," in Ismail, *Hudud in Malaysia*, 13–21.

129 Stark, *Constructing an Islamic Model*, 59.

130 Hong Qu, "Impact of Islamic Family Law on Malaysian Muslim Women," http://www.asianscholarhsip.org/publications/papers/Qu%20hong-Impact%20 %Islamic%20Familiy%20Law.doc (accessed October 19, 2004).

131 Zaenah Anwar, "Islamisation and its Impact on Laws and the Law Making Process in Malaysia," http://www.whrnet.org/fundamentalisms/docs/doc-wsf-zainah-malaysia-0311.rtf (accessed October 18, 2004).

132 Ibid.

133 Jan Stark, *Constructing an Islamic Model*, 60.

134 Ibid.

135 Ibid., 66.

136 Ibid., 68.

137 Ibid., 63.

138 International Crisis Group, "Aceh: Escalating Tension," Asia Briefing No. 4 (December 7, 2000), 2.

139 See S. M. Amin, 1980, "Sejenak Meninjau Aceh, Serambi Mekkah," in Suny, *Bunga Rampai*, 45–102.

140 See Kasimin, *Religion and Social Change*, 150–52; Azyumardi Azra, *Renaisans Islam Asia Tenggara: Sejarah Wacana dan Kekuasaan* (Bandung: Rosdakarya, 1999), 41. See also, Anthony Reid, "Introduction," in *The Making of an Islamic Political*

Discourse in Southeast Asia, ed. Anthony Reid (Victoria: Center of Southeast Asia, 1993), 1–16.

141 Bustamam-Ahmad, "Kontribusi Daerah Aceh," 150–54.

142 Karel A. Steenbrink, *Beberapa Aspek Tentang Islam di Indonesia Abad ke-19* (Jakarta: Bulan Bintang, 1984), 4.

143 Saby, "Islam and Social Change," 18.

144 Ibid., 20.

145 Mudzhar, *Fatwa-Fatwa*, 15.

146 Ibid.

147 A. Mukti Ali, *An Introduction to the Government of Acheh's Sultanate* (Yogyakarta: Jajasan Nida, 1970), 7.

148 Ibid.

149 Syed Muhammad Naquib Al-Attas, *A Commentary on the Hujjat al-Siddiq of Nur al-Din al-Raniri* (Kuala Lumpur: Ministry of Culture Malaysia, 1986), 5.

150 See Oman Fatahurahman, *Tanbîh al-Masyî, Menyoal Wahdatul Wujud: Kasus Abdurrauf Singkel di Aceh Abad 17* (Bandung: École Française d'Extrème-Orient and Mizan, 1999).

151 Al-Attas, *Commentary on the Hujjat al-Siddiq*, 6.

152 See Peunoh Daly, *Hukum Perkawinan Islam: Suatu Studi Perbandingan dalam Kalangan Ahlus-Sunnah dan Negara-negara Islam* (Jakarta: Bulan Bintang, 1988), 28–29.

153 Ali, "Introduction to the Government," 7.

154 On this topic, see Denys Lombard, *Kerajaan Aceh: Jaman Sultan Iskandar Muda (1607–1636)*, trans. Winarsih Arifin (Jakarta: Balai Pustaka 1986); Al-Attas, *Commentary on the Hujjat al-Siddiq*, 7; Hing, *Sultanate of Aceh*, 14–15; Saby, *Islam and Social Change*, 32–39.

155 Al-Attas, *Commentary on the Hujjat al-Siddiq*, 7.

156 Saby, *Islam and Social Change*, 32. See also Idem., "The *Ulama* in Aceh: A Brief Historical Survey," *Studia Islamika* 8, no. 1 (2001), 1–54.

157 Saby, *Islam and Social Change*, 68.

158 Azyumardi Azra, *Menuju Masyarakat Madani: Gagasan, Fakta, dan Tantangan* (Bandung: Rosdakarya, 1999), 29.

159 Saby, *Islam and Social Change*, 72.

160 Azra, *Menuju Masyarakat Madani*, 29.

161 Saby, *Islam and Social Change*, 72.

162 Ibid., 72.

163 Martin van Bruinessen, *Kitab Kuning Pesantren dan Tarekat: Tradisi-Tradisi Islam di Indonesia* (Bandung: Mizan, 1999), 113.

164 Al-Attas, *Commentary on the Hujjat al-Siddiq*, 25.

165 Azyumardi Azra, "Tanbih al-Masyi; Otentisitas Kepakaran Abdurrauf Singkel," in *Tanbih Al-Masyi*, ed. Oman Fathurrahman (Bandung: Mizan, 1999), 15.

166 Cited in Kaptein, *Muhimmât al-Nafâ'is*, xii.

167 On *dayah* in Aceh, see M. Hasbi Amiruddin, *Ulama Dayah: Pengawal Agama Masyarakat Aceh*, trans. Kamaruzzaman (Lhokseumawe: Nadiya Foundation, 2003).

168 Ali, *Introduction to the Government*, 22. See also J. F. Holleman, ed., *Van Vollenhoven on Indonesia Adat Law* (The Hague: Koninklijk Instituut Voor Taal-, Land en Volkenkunde, 1981), 54–122.

169 C. Snouck C. Hurgronje, *The Acehnese* (Leiden: E. J. Brill, 1906), 72.

170 Ismuha, "Ulama Aceh Dalam Perspektif Sejarah," in *Agama dan Perubahan Sosial*, ed. Taufik Abdullah (Jakarta: Raja Grafindo Persada, 1996), 6; Idem., "Adat and Agama di Aceh," Working Paper No. 16. (Darussalam: Pusat Latihan Penelitian Ilmu-ilmu Sosial, 1983), 9.

171 See Luthfi Auni, "The Decline of the Islamic Empire of Aceh" (master's thesis, McGill University, 1993), 8–9.

172 Ali, *An Introduction to the Government*, 24. For the Indonesian context, see Ratno Lukito, *Islamic Law and Adat Encounter: The Experience of Indonesia* (Jakarta: Logos 2001); Idem., "Law and Politics in Post Independence Indonesia: A Case Study of Religious and Adat Courts," *Studia Islamika* 6, no. 2 (1999): 63–86.

173 See generally, Snouck. C. Hurgronje, *Aceh: Rakyat Adat dan Adat Istiadatnya*, trans. Sutan Maimoen (Jakarta: INIS, 1997), 67–91.

174 Taufik Abdullah, *Islam Masyarakat: Pantulan Sejarah Indonesia* (Jakarta: LP3ES, 1996), 168.

175 Ibid., 12.

176 Ali, 1970, *Introduction to the Government*, 12.

177 Ibid., 13.

178 See Saby, *Islam and Social Change*, 110.

179 Ali, *Introduction to the Government*, 14.

180 Akh. Minhaji, "Ahmad Hassan and Islamic Legal Reform in Indonesia (1887–1959)" (PhD diss., McGill University, 1997), 51.

181 See Amirul Hadi, "Aceh and the Portuguese: A Study of the Struggle of Islam in Southeast Asia," (master's thesis, McGill University, 1992), 81.

182 Hurgronje, *The Acehnese*, 166.

183 Minhaji, *Ahmad Hassan*, 56.

184 International Crisis Group, "Islamic Law and Criminal Justice in Aceh," Asia Report No. 117, July 31, 2006.

185 See Saifuddin Anshari, "Islam or the Pancasila as the Basis of the State," in *Readings on Islam in Southeast Asia*, eds. Ahmad Ibrahim, et al. (Singapore: ISEAS, 1996), 221–28.

186 Lukito, *Islamic Law*, 76–77.

187 Lukito, "Law and Politics," 69. See also, Daniel S. Lev, *Islamic Courts in Indonesia: A Study in the Political Basis of Legal Institutions* (Berkeley: University of California Press, 1972).

188 Sujitno and Achmad, *Aceh*, 56.

189 Feith and Castles, *Pemikiran Politik Indonesia*, 209–10; see also Taufik Abdullah, "Teungku Daud Beureueh: Pejuang Kemerdekaan yang Berontak," *Tempo*, August 24, 2003, 26–27, cited in *Tamaddun dan Sejarah: Etnografi Kekerasan di Aceh*, ed. Hasanuddin Yusuf Adan (Yogyakarta: Prismasophie Press, 2003), 55–71.

190 Abdullah, "Teungku Daud Beureueh," 31.

191 See Anthony Reid, "Perlawanan dalam Sejarah Nanggroe Aceh Darussalam," *Tempo*, August, 24, 2003, 39. For Hasan's view on nationalism, see Tengku Hasan di Tiro, "Nasionalisme Indonesia," in *Mengapa Sumatera Menggugat*, ed. Yusra Habib Abdul Ghani (Biro Penerangan Acheh-Sumatra National Liberation Front, 2000), 41–67.

192 Amnesty International, "'Shock Therapy': Restoring Order in Aceh, 1989–1993," London, August 02, 1993, http://acehnet.tripod.com/shock.htm

193 Interview with Safwan Idris, July 1999.

194 Tengku Hasan di Tiro, *The Price of Freedom: The Unfinished Diary of Tengku Hasan di Tiro* (National Liberation Front Acheh Sumatra Information Department, 1984), 4.

195 Ibid., 10.

196 Ibid., 11. See also Idem., "Konsep-Konsep Kunci Ideologi Acheh Merdeka," *Suara Acheh Merdeka* 7 (1995): 29–37.

197 Tengku Hasan di Tiro, "Violations of Human Rights by Indonesia Acheh/Sumatra and the Acehnese Legitimate Struggle for Independence from Indonesia," *Agam: Madjallah Angkatan Atjeh Meurdehka* 40 (1991), 19.

198 Amnesty International, "'Shock Therapy.'"

199 Human Rights Watch, "Indonesia: The War in Aceh," A Human Rights Watch Report, vol. 13, no. 4, August 2001, 5.

200 See Kamaruzzaman Bustamam-Ahmad, *Wajah Baru Islam di Indonesia* (Yogyakarta: UII Press, 2004).

201 Human Rights Watch, "The War in Aceh," 7.

202 International Crisis Group, "Aceh: Can Autonomy Stem the Conflict," 11.

203 Human Rights Watch, "The War in Aceh," 8.

204 Amnesty International, "'Shock Therapy.'"

205 International Crisis Group, "Aceh: Escalating Tension," 4.

206 Al-Chaidar, et al., *Aceh Bersimbah Darah: Mengungkap Penerapan Status Daerah Operasi Militer (DOM) di Aceh 1989–1998* (Jakarta: al-Kautsar, 1999), 106; Kamaruzzaman Bustamam-Ahmad, *Islam Historis*, 296–97.

207 Interview with M. Hasbi Amiruddin, May 2004; interview with Al-Yasa Abubakar, June 2004; interview with Yusuf Hasan, May 2004.

208 See generally, Amirul Hadi, *Islam and State in Sumatra: A Study of Seventeenth-Century Aceh* (Leiden: E. J. Brill 2004); Syah and Hakiem, *Keistimewaan Aceh dalam Lintasan Sejarah*, 11–59.

209 International Crisis Group, "Aceh: Can Autonomy Stem the Conflict," 10.

210 Michelle Ann Miller, "What's Special About Special Autonomy in Aceh" (paper presented at Conference on the Historical Background of the Aceh Problem, Asia Research Institute, National University Singapore, May, 28–29, 2004), 11.

211 Ibid., 11.

212 Staffan Bodemar, "Conflict in Aceh, Indonesia: Background, Current Situation, and Future Perspective," unpublished paper, March 2004, 30. See also Michelle Ann Miller, "The Naggroe Aceh Darussalam Law: A Serious Response to Acehnese Separatism?" *Asian Ethnicity* 15, no. 3 (2004), 340–43.

213 Lily Zakiyah Munir, "Has Shari'a Brought Justice?" *The Jakarta Post*, March 17, 2003.

214 Interviews with Al-Yasa Abubakar, May 2005; Yusuf Hasan, May 2004; Marlinda Puteh, May 2004.

215 Interviews with Iskandar Budiman, May 2004; Hasanuddin Yusuf Adan, May 2004.

216 See Al-Yasa Abubakar, *Tanya Jawab Pelaksanaan Syariat Islam di Provinsi Nanggroe Aceh Darussalam* (Banda Aceh: Dinas Syariat Islam, 2003), 18–23.

217 Sudiyotomo, "ABRI Mendukung Penuh," in Syah and Hakiem, *Keistimewaan Aceh*, 165.

218 Sajid Soetjoro, "Tidak Cukup Dengan Pendekatan Keamanan," in Syah and Hakiem, eds., *Keistimewaan Aceh*, 173–75.

219 International Crisis Group, "Aceh: Can Autonomy Stem the Conflict," 14.

220 Ibid., 14.

221 Interviews with Al-Yasa Abubakar, May 2004; Yusuf Hasan, May 2004; Nurjannah Ismail, May 2004; Marlinda Puteh, May 2004; Iskandar Budiman, May 2004.

222 Interviews with Iskandar Budiman, May 2004; Hasanuddin Yusuf Adan, May 2004; Mohd. Abdurrahman, June 2004.

223 Interviews with M. Hasbi Amiruddin, May 2004; Helmy Hass, July 2004; M. Adli Abdullah, July 2004.

224 A number of people are suspected of being *koruptor*, such as Abdullah Puteh, the governor of Aceh.

225 See Wahid and Nurrohman, "Dimensi Fundamentalisme," 34–59.

226 For further details, see Kamaruzzaman Bustamam-Ahmad, "Metaformosis Pemikiran Intelektual Muda NU: Suatu Pandangan dari Outsider NU," *Millah* 4, no. 2 (2004): 111–26; Idem., *Wajah Baru Islam di Indonesia*, 51–100; Zuly Qodir, "Wajah Islam Liberal di Indonesia: Sebuah Penjajagan Awal," *Al-Jamiah* 40, no. 2 (2002), 325–53.

227 Azyumardi Azra, "Belum ada Negara Sebagai Acuan Pelaksanaan Syariat Islam," in *Syariat Islam Yes, Syariat Islam No: dilema Piagam Jakarta dalam amademen UUD 1945*, A. Syafii Maarif, et al. (Jakarta: Paramadina, 2001), 184. See also, Azyumardi Azra, "Communal Riots in Indonesia: The Decline of Indonesian Nationalism and the Rise of Separatism," in *Communal Conflict in Contemporary Indonesia*, eds. Murni Jamal and Klaus Pahler (Jakarta: The Center for Language and Culture and The Konrad Adeneur Foundation, 2002), 82–87; Idem., *Konflik Baru Antar Peradaban: Globalisasi, Radikalisme dan Pluralitas* (Jakarta: Grafiti, 2002) 126–32.

228 Interview with Irwandar, May 2004.

229 Interview with Nurdin, July 2004.

230 Suraiya Kamaruzzaman, "Women and Syariah in Aceh," *Inside Indonesia*, July–September, 2004, 9.

231 Interviews with Ali Jauhary, May 2004; Nurjannah Ismail, May 2004.

232 Interview with Nurjannah Ismail, May 2004.

233 Interview with Ali Jauhary, May 2004.

234 Interview with Marlinda Puteh, May 2004.

235 Interview with Al-Yasa Abubakar, May 2004.

236 Interview with Marlinda Puteh, May 2004.

237 Interview with Al-Yasa Abubakar, May 2004.

238 Interview with Yusuf Hasan, May 2004.

239 Miller, "Nanggroe Aceh Darussalam Law," 342; Rodd McGibbon, *Secessionist Challenges in Aceh and Papua: Is Special Autonomy the Solution?* Policy Studies 10 (Washington, DC: East-West Center Washington, 2004), 29.

240 Miller, 2004, "Nanggroe Aceh Darussalam Law," 343.

241 The five "pillars" or principles of Pancasila are: belief in one supreme god, just and civilized humanism, the unity of Indonesia, democracy, and social welfare.

242 See, e.g., Miller, "Nanggroe Aceh Darussalam Law," 348–51.

243 Bustamam-Ahmad, *Islam Historis*, 318–19.

244 Miller, "Nanggroe Aceh Darussalam Law," 345.

245 Muhammad Yusof Ismail, "Buddhism in a Muslim State: Theravada Practices and Religious Life in Kelantan" (paper presented at the Workshop Proceedings "A Plural Peninsula: Historical Interactions among the Thai, Malays, Chinese and Others," Nakhon Sri Thammarat, Walailak University, February 5–7, 2004), 96.

246 Hasan, "Syariat Islam yang Kami Pahami," in *Syariat di Wilayah Syariat: Pernik-Pernik Islam di Nanggroes Aceh Darussalam*, ed. Fairus M. Nur Ibr (Banda Aceh: Dinas Syariat Islam, 2002), 274.

247 Frietz R. Tambunan, "Pelaksanaan Syariat Islam: Sebuah Refleksi Berdasarkan Pengalaman Gerejan (Katolik)," in Fairus M. Nur Ibr, ed., *Syariat di Wilayah Syariat*, 288–89.

BIBLIOGRAPHY

Abdullah, Taufik. "*Adat* and Islam: An Examination of Conflict in Minangkabau." *Indonesia* 2 (1966): 1–24.

———. *Islam Masyarakat: Pantulan Sejarah Indonesia.* Jakarta: LP3ES, 1996.

———. "Some Notes on the Kaba Tjindua Mato: An Example of Minangkabau Traditional Literature." *Indonesia* 9 (1970): 1–22.

———. "Teungku Daud Beureueh: Pejuang Kemerdekaan yang Berontak." *Tempo,* August, 24, 2003.

Abubakar, Al-Yasa. *Tanya Jawab Pelaksanaan Syariat Islam di Provinsi Nanggroe Aceh Darussalam.* Banda Aceh: Dinas Syariat Islam, 2003.

Adan, Hasanuddin Yusuf, ed. *Tamaddun dan Sejarah: Etnografi Kekerasan di Aceh* [Civilization and History: The Ethnography of Violence in Aceh]. Yogyakarta: Prismasophie Press, 2003.

Ahmad, Salbiah. "*Zina* and Rape under the Syariah Criminal Code (II) Bill 1993 (Kelantan)." In *Hudud in Malaysia: The Issues at Stake,* edited by Rose Ismail. Selangor: Ilmiah Publishers, 2002.

Ahmad, Shukri. "Implikasi Pengaruh Ulama Terhadap Halatuju Perubahan Pemikiran Politik Masyarakat Islam Wilayah Utara Semenanjung Malaysia Dari 1950-an Hingga 1990-an" [The Implications of *Ulama's* Influence in a Changing Society's Political Thought in North Malaysia from 1950 to 1990]. *Journal of Ushuluddin* 14 (2001): 97–122.

Ali, A. Mukti. *An Introduction to the Government of Aceh's Sultanate.* Yogyakarta: Jajasan Nida, 1970.

Amin, S. M. "Sejenak Meninjau Aceh, Serambi Mekkah." In *Bunga Rampai tentang Aceh,* edited by Ismail Suny, 45–102. Jakarta: Bhratara, 1980.

Amiq. "Two Fatwâs on Jihâd against the Dutch Colonization in Indonesia: A Prosopographical Approach to the Study of Fatwâ." *Studia Islamika* 5, no. 3 (1998): 77–124.

Amiruddin, M. Hasbi. *Ulama Dayah: Pengawal Agama Masyarakat Aceh,* trans. by Kamaruzzaman. Lhokseumawe: Nadiya Foundation. 2003.

Amnesty International. "'Shock Therapy': Restoring Order in Aceh, 1989–1993." August 2, 1993, http://acehnet.tripod.com/shock.htm.

Anderson, J. N. D. *Islamic Law in the Modern World.* New York: New York University Press, 1959.

Ansari, Zafar Ishaq. "Foreword." In *Theories of Islamic Law: The Methodology of Ijtihâd,* edited by Imran Ahsan Khan Nyazee. Pakistan: International Institute of Islamic Thought and Islamic Research Institute, 1994.

Anshari, Saifuddin. "Islam or the Panca Sila as the Basis of the State." In *Readings on Islam in Southeast Asia*, edited by Ahmad Ibrahim, et al., 221–28. Singapore: ISEAS, 1985.

Anwar, Syamsul. "Islamic Jurisprudence of Christian-Muslim Relations: Toward a Reinterpretation." *Al-Jamiah* 61 (1997): 128–53.

Anwar, Zaenah. "Islamisation and its Impact on Laws and the Law Making Process in Malaysia," December 2003, http://www.whrnet.org/fundamentalisms/docs/ doc-wsf-zainah-malaysia-0311.rtf (accessed October 18, 2004).

Arfa, Faisar Ananda. *Sejarah Pembentukan Hukum Islam: Studi Kritis tentang Hukum Islam di Barat*. Jakarta: Pustaka Firdaus, 1996.

Atjeh, Aboebakar. "Tentang Name Aceh." In *Bunga Rampai tentang Aceh*, edited by Ismail Suny, 15–26. Jakarta: Bhratara, 1980.

Attas, Muhammad Naquib Al-. *A Commentary on the Hujjat al-Siddiq of Nur al-Din al-Raniri*. Kuala Lumpur: Ministry of Culture, 1986.

Auni, Luthfi. "The Decline of the Islamic Empire of Aceh." Master's thesis, McGill University, 1993.

Ayyub, Mahmoud. "Sulit, Menerapkan Sistem Politik Berbasis Syariah" [Difficult to Apply Political System Based on *Shariah*]. *Tashwirul Afkar* 13 (2002): 121–25.

Azizy, A. Qodri. *Ekletisme Hukum Nasional: Kompetisi Antara Hukum Islam dan Hukum Umum*. Yogyakarta: Gama Media, 2002.

———. "Juristic Differences (*Ikhtilaf*) in Islamic Law: Its Meaning, Early Discussions, and Reasons (a Lesson for Contemporary Characteristics)." *Al-Jamiah* 39, no. 2 (2001).

Azra, Azyumardi. "Belum ada Negara Sebagai Acuan Pelaksanaan Syariat Islam." In *Syariat Islam Yes, Syariat Islam No: dilema Piagam Jakarta dalam amademen UUD 1945*, A. Syafii Maarif, et al. Jakarta: Paramadina, 2001.

———. "Communal Riots in Indonesia: The Decline of Indonesian Nationalism and the Rise of Separatism." In *Communal Conflict in Contemporary Indonesia*, edited by Murni Jamal and Klaus Pahler. Jakarta: The Center for Language and Culture and the Konrad Adeneur Foundation, 2002.

———. *Konflik Baru Antar Peradaban: Globalisasi, Radikalisme dan Pluralitas*. Jakarta: Grafiti, 2002.

———. *Menuju Masyarakat Madani: Gagasan, Fakta, dan Tantangan*. Bandung: Rosdakarya, 1999.

———. *Pendidikan Islam: Tradisi dan Modernisasi Menuju Milenium Baru*. Jakarta: Logos, 1999.

———. *Renaisans Islam Asia Tenggara: Sejarah Wacana dan Kekuasaan*. Bandung: Rosdakarya, 1999.

————. "*Tanbih al-Masyi*: Otentisitas Kepakaran Abdurrauf Singkel." In *Tanbih Al-Masyi*, edited by Oman Fathurrahman. Bandung: Mizan, 1999.

Baderin, Mashood A. *International Human Rights and Islamic Law.* Oxford: Oxford University Press, 2003.

Bodemar, Staffan. "Conflict in Aceh, Indonesia: Background, Current Situation, and Future Perspective." Unpublished paper, March 2004.

Bowen, John R. "'You May Not Give it Away': How Social Norms Shape Islamic Law in Contemporary Indonesian Jurisprudence." *Islamic Law and Society* 5, no. 3 (1998): 382–408.

Bruinessen, Martin van. *Kitab Kuning Pesantren dan Tarekat: Tradisi-Tradisi Islam di Indonesia.* Bandung: Mizan, 1999.

Bustamam-Ahmad, Kamaruzzaman. "Hubungan Agama dan Negara" [The Relationship between Religion and the State]. *Pemikir* 30 (2002): 93–119.

————. *Islam Historis: Dinamika Studi Islam di Indonesia* [Dynamics of Islamic Studies in Indonesia]. Yogyakarta: Galang Press, 2002.

————. "Konsep Negara Era Moden" [The Concept of State in the Modern Era]. *Pemikir* 31 (2003): 233–58.

————. "Kontribusi Daerah Aceh Terhadap Perkembangan Awal Hukum Islam di Indonesia" [Aceh's Contribution to the Early Development of Islamic Law in Indonesia]. *Al-Jamiah: Journal of Islamic Studies* 64 (1999): 143–75.

————. "Menakar Harga Kemarahan Orang Aceh: Ethnografi Kekerasan di Indonesia" [The Cost of Acehnese Anger: The Ethnography of Violence in Indonesia]. In *Tamaddun dan Sejarah: Etnografi Kekerasan di Aceh* [Civilization and History: The Ethnography of Violence in Aceh], edited by Hasanuddin Yusuf Adan, 9–38. Yogyakarta: Ar-Ruzz, 2003.

————. "Metaformosis Pemikiran Intelektual Muda NU: Suatu Pandangan dari Outsider NU." *Millah* 4, no. 2 (2004): 111–26.

————. "Perdebatan Mengenai Negara Islam" [Debate on the Islamic State]. *Siasah,* November 26–27, 2001.

————. "Relasi Ugama [Islam] dan Politik" [The Relationship between Religion and Politics]. *Siasah,* October 26–29, 2001.

————. *Satu Dasawarwa the Clash of Civilizations* [The Tenth Year of the Clash of Civilizations]. Yogyakarta: Ar-Ruzz, 2003.

————. *Wajah Baru Islam di Indonesia.* Yogyakarta: UII Press, 2004.

Case, William. *Politics in Southeast Asia: Democracy or Less.* Richmond, London: Curzon Press, 2002.

Chaidar, Al-, et al. *Aceh Bersimbah Darah: Mengungkap Penerapan Status Daerah Operasi Militer (DOM) di Aceh 1989–1998.* Jakarta: Al-Kautsar, 1999.

Choudhury, G. W. *Islam and the Modern Muslim World*. Kuala Lumpur: WHS Publications, 1993.

Constable, Olivia Remie. "Reconsidering the Origin of the Funduq." *Studia Islamica* 92 (2001): 195–96.

Dahlan, Abdul Azis, et al., eds. *Ensiklopedi Hukum Islam*. 6 vols. Jakarta: Ichtiar van Hoeve, 1997.

Daly, Peunoh. *Hukum Perkawinan Islam: Suatu Studi Perbandingan dalam Kalangan Ahlus-Sunnah dan Negara-negara Islam*. Jakarta: Bulan Bintang, 1988.

"DAP opposes *hudud* laws." *New Straits Times*, April 10, 1992

Dengel, Holk H. *Darul Islam dan Kartosuwirjo* [The Islamic State and Kartosuwirjo]. Jakarta: Sihar Harapan, 1995.

Dhofier, Zamahksyari. *Tradisi Pesantren: Studi tentang Pandangan Hidup Kyai*. [The Pesantren Tradition: A Study of the Life View of Kyai]. Jakarta: LP3ES, 1982.

Dijk, C. Van. "Is God a Gangster? Political and Religious Authority and Religious Sentiments." Paper presented at an IIAS and ISIM Workshop on "Fatwas and the Dissemination of Religious Authority in Indonesia," Leiden, October 31, 2002.

Dja'far, Muhammad Alfian. "Independensi Mahkamah Syariah Nanggroew Aceh Darussalam" [The Islamic Courts' Independence in Nanggroe Aceh Darussalam]. Bachelor's thesis, State Institute of Islamic Studies, Yogyakarta, 2003.

Dobbin, Christine. "Islamic Revivalism in Minangkabau at the Turn of the Nineteenth Century." *Modern Asian Studies* 8, no. 3 (1974): 319–45.

Drewes, G. W. J. "New Light on the Coming of Islam to Indonesia." In *Readings on Islam in Southeast Asia*, edited by Ahmad Ibrahim, et al., 7–19. Singapore: Institute of Southeast Asian Studies, 1985.

Faruqi, Maysam J. Al-. "*Umma*: The Orientalist and The Qur'anic Concept of Identity." *Journal of Islamic Studies* 16, no. 1 (2005): 1–34.

Fathurahman, Oman. *Tanbih al-Masyi, Menyoal Wahdatul Wujud: Kasus Abdurrauf Singkel di Aceh Abad 17*. Bandung: École Française d'Extrème-Orient and Mizan, 1999.

Fatimi, S. Q. *Islam Comes to Malaysia*. Singapore: Malaysia Sociological Research Institute Ltd., 1963.

Feith, Herbert and Lance Castles, eds. *Pemikiran Politik Indonesia 1945–1965* [Indonesian Political Thinking, 1945–1965], trans. Min Yubahar. Jakarta: LP3ES, 1988.

Fernando, Joseph M. "The Position of Islam in the Constitution of Malaysia." *Journal of Southeast Asian Studies* 37, no. 2 (2006): 249–66.

Gleave, Robert. *Inevitable Doubt: Two Theories of Shi'i Jurisprudence.* Leiden: E. J. Brill, 2000.

Gleave, Robert and E. Kermeli, eds. *Islamic Law: Theory and Practice.* New York: I. B. Tauris, 1997.

Guinn, David E., et al., eds. *Religion and Law in the Global Village.* Atlanta: Scholars Press, 1999.

Hadi, Amirul. "Aceh and the Portuguese: A Study of the Struggle of Islam in Southeast Asia." Master's thesis, McGill University, 1992.

————. *Islam and State in Sumatra: A Study of Seventeenth-Century Aceh.* Leiden: E. J. Brill, 2004.

Hallaq, Wael B. *A History of Islamic Legal Theories: An Introduction to Sunni Usul Fiqh.* Cambridge: Cambridge University Press, 1997.

————. "On the Origins of the Controversy about the Existence of Mujtahids and the Gate of Ijtihad." *Studia Islamica* 63 (1986): 129–41.

————. "Was the Gate of Ijtihad Closed?" *International Journal of Middle East Studies* 16 (1984): 3–41.

Hamilton, Alexander. *A New Account of the East Indies, Being the Observations and Remarks of Capt. Alexander Hamilton Who Spent His Time There* (Edinburgh: John Mofman, 1727).

Hamzah, Tengku Razaleigh. "The Semangat 46 View." In *Hudud in Malaysia,* edited by Rose Ismail. Selangor: Ilmiah Publishers, 2002.

Hamzah, Wan Arfah and Ramy Bulan. *An Introduction to the Malaysian Legal System.* Selangor: Fajar Bakti, 2003.

Hasan. "Syariat Islam yang Kami Pahami." In *Syariat di Wilayah Syariat: Pernik-Pernik Islam di Nanggroe Aceh Darussalam,* edited by Fairus M. Nur Ibr. Banda Aceh: Dinas Syariat Islam, 2002.

Hassan, Abdullah Alwi Haji. *The Administration of Islamic Law in Kelantan.* Kuala Lumpur: Dewan Bahasa dan Pustaka, 1996.

Hassan, Ahmad. *Pintu Ijtihad Sebelum Tertutup,* trans. by Agah Garnadi. Bandung: Pustaka, 1994.

Hefner, Robert W. *Civil Islam: Muslim and Democratization in Indonesia.* Princeton: Princeton University Press, 2000.

Hing, Lee Kam. *The Sultanate of Aceh: Relations with the British 1760–1824.* Kuala Lumpur: Oxford University of Press, 1995.

Holleman, J. F., ed. *Van Vollenhoven on Indonesia Adat Law.* The Hague: Koninklijk Instituut Voor Taal-, Land- en Volkenkunde, 1981.

Hooker, M. B., ed. "Introduction: Islamic Law in South-East Asia." *Australian Journal of Asian Law* 4, no. 3 (2002): 213–31.

————. *Islam Mazhab Indonesia: Fatwa-Fatwa dan Perubahan Sosial* [Islam Indonesia Islamic Legal Thought: *Fatwas* and Social Change]. Bandung: Teraju Mizan, 2003.

————. *Islam in South-East Asia*. Leiden: E. J. Brill, 1983.

————. *Islamic Law in South-East Asia*. Singapore: Oxford University Press, 1984.

————. "The State and Shari'ah in Indonesia, 1945–1995." In *Indonesia: Law and Society*, edited by Timothy Lindsey. Sydney: Federation Press, 1999.

Hourani, George F. "Islamic and Non-Islamic Origins of Mu'tazilite Ethical Rationalism." *International Journal of Middle East Studies* 7, no. 1 (1976), 59–87.

————. "Joseph Schacht, 1902–69," *Journal of the American Oriental Society* 90, no. 2 (1970), 163–67.

Human Rights Watch. "Indonesia: The War in Aceh." A Human Rights Watch Report, vol. 13, no. 4, August 2001.

Humphreys, R. Stephen. *Islamic History: A Framework for Inquiry*. Princeton: Princeton University Press, 1991.

Hurgronje, C. S. *The Acehnese*. Leiden: E. J. Brill, 1906.

Ibrahim, Rosli. "Isu Malaysia Negara Islam: Antara Kenyataan dan Kejahilan" [The Malaysian Issue on the Islamic State: Between Reality and Stupidity]. *Siasah*, Bil. 7, November 29–30, 2001.

International Crisis Group. "Aceh: Can Autonomy Stem the Conflict?" Asia Briefing No. 18, June 27, 2001.

————. "Aceh: Escalating Tension." Asia Briefing No. 4, December 7, 2000.

————. "Islamic Law and Criminal Justice in Aceh." Asia Report No. 117, July 31, 2006.

"Islamic State Document" (ISD), prepared by PAS, November 12, 2003, http://www. parti-pas.org/IslamicStateDocument.php (accessed October 14, 2004).

Ismail, Muhammad Yusof. "Buddhism in a Muslim State: Theravada Practices and Religious Life in Kelantan." Workshop Proceedings of "A Plural Peninsula: Historical Interactions among the Thai, Malays, Chinese and Others," Nakhon Sri Thammarat, Walailak University, February 5–7, 2004.

Ismuha. "Adat and Agama di Aceh." Working Paper No. 16. Darussalam: Pusat Latihan Penelitian Ilmu-ilmu Sosial, 1983.

————. "Ulama Aceh Dalam Perspektif Sejarah." In *Agama dan Perubahan Sosial*, edited by Taufik Abdullah. Jakarta: Raja Grafindo Persada, 1996.

Johansen, Baber. *Contingency in a Sacred Law: Legal and Ethical Norms in the Muslim Fiqh*. Leiden: E. J. Brill, 1999.

Ka'bah, Rifyal. "Pluralisme dalam Perspektif Syariah" [Pluralism in *Shariah* Perspective]. *Mimbar Hukum* 5 (2001): 7–14.

Kamali, Mohammad Hashim. *Punishment in Islamic Law: An Enquiry into the Hudud Bill of Kelantan.* Kuala Lumpur: Ilmiah Publishers, 2000.

Kamaruzzaman, Suraiya. "Women and Syariah in Aceh." *Inside Indonesia,* July–September, 2004.

Kaptein, Nico. "Acceptance, Approval and Aggression: Some Fatwas Concerning the Colonial Administration in the Dutch East Indies." *Al-Jamiah* 38, no. 2 (2000): 297–330.

———. *The Muhimmât al-Nafâ'is: A Bilingual Meccan Fatwa Collection for Indonesian Muslims from the End of the Nineteenth Century.* Jakarta: INIS, 1997.

Kasimin, Amran. *Religion and Social Change among the Indigenous People of the Malay Peninsula.* Kuala Lumpur: Dewan Bahasa dan Pustaka Kementerian Pendidikan Malaysia, 1991.

Khallaf, Abdul Wahhab. *'Ilm Ushul al-Fiqh.* Beirut: Dar al-Qalam, 1978.

Kim, Khoo Kay. "Introduction." In *An Expedition to Trengganu and Kelantan 1895,* edited by Hugh Clifford. Kuala Lumpur: MBRAS, 1992.

Layish, Aharon. "Notes on Joseph Schacht's Contribution to the Study of Islamic Law." *British Journal of Middle Eastern Studies* 9, no. 2 (1982): 132–40.

Lev, Daniel S. *Islamic Courts in Indonesia: A Study in the Political Bases of Legal Institutions.* Berkeley: University of California Press, 1972.

Liow, Joseph. "Deconstructing Political Islam in Malaysia: UMNO's Responses to PAS' Religio-Political Dialectic." Working Paper, No. 45. Singapore: Institute of Defence and Strategic Studies, 2003.

Lombard, Denys. *Kerajaan Aceh: Jaman Sultan Iskandar Muda (1607–1636),* trans. by Winarsih Arifin. Jakarta: Balai Pustaka, 1986.

Lukito, Ratno. *Islamic Law and Adat Encounter: The Experience of Indonesia.* Jakarta: Logos, 2001.

———. "Law and Politics in Post Independence Indonesia: A Case Study of Religious and *Adat* Courts." *Studia Islamika* 6, no. 2 (1999): 63–86.

"Mahathir, Dr. to Aziz: try *hudud* laws now." *New Straits Times,* April 17, 1992.

"Mahathir: Malaysia is a 'fundamentalist state,'" CNN.com/World, June 18, 2002, http://archives.cnn.com/2002/WORLD/asiapcf/southeast/06/18/malaysia. mahathir (accessed October 15, 2004).

Mahmood, Tahir, ed. *Human Rights in Islamic Law.* New Delhi: Genuine Publications, 1993.

Mas'udi, Masdar F. "Hak Azasi Manusia dalam Islam" [Human Rights in Islam]. In *Diseminasi Hak Asasi Manusia: Perspektif dan Aksi* [The Dissemination of Human Rights: Perspective and Action], edited by E. Shobirin Nadj and Naning Mardiniah, 63–72. Jakarta: LP3ES, 2000.

Masud, Abdurrahman. "Why the *Pesantren* in Indonesia Remains Unique and Stronger." In *Islamic Studies in ASEAN: Presentations of an International Seminar*, edited by Isma-ae Alee, et al., 191–202. Pattani: Prince of Songkla University, 2000.

Masud, Mohd. Khalid, et al., eds. *Islamic Legal Interpretation*. Cambridge, MA: Harvard University Press, 1996.

Mayer, Ann Elizabeth. *Islam and Human Rights: Tradition and Politics*. Boulder, CO: Westview Press, 1991.

—————. *Property, Social Structure and Law in the Modern Middle East*. Albany: State University of New York Press, 1985.

—————. "Religious Legitimacy and Constitutionalism: The Saudi Basic Law and the Moroccan Constitution Compared." In *Religion and Law in the Global Village*, edited by David E. Guinn, et al., 81–97. Atlanta: Scholars Press, 1999.

McGibbon, Rodd. *Secessionist Challenges in Aceh and Papua: Is Special Autonomy the Solution?* Policy Studies 10. Washington, DC: East-West Center Washington, 2004.

Mehden, Fred R. von der. "Malaysia: Islam and Multiethnic Polities." In *Islam in Asia: Religion, Politics, and Society*, edited by John L. Esposito. New York: Oxford University Press, 1987.

Miller, Michelle Ann. "The Nanggroe Aceh Darussalam Law: A Serious Response to Acehnese Separatism." *Asian Ethnicity* 15, no. 3 (2004): 333–51.

—————. "What's Special About Special Autonomy in Aceh." Paper presented at the Conference on the Historical Background of the Aceh Problem, Asia Research Institute, National University Singapore, May, 28–29, 2004.

Minhaji, Akh. "Ahmad Hassan and Islamic Legal Reform in Indonesia (1887–1959)." PhD diss., McGill University, 1997.

—————. *Ahmad Hassan and Islamic Legal Reform in Indonesia (1887–1959)*. Yogyakarta: Kurnia Kalam Semesta Press, 2001.

—————. *Kontroversi Pembentukan Hukum Islam: Kontribusi Joseph Schacht*. Yogyakarta: UII Press, 2001.

—————. "Modern Trends in Islamic Law: Notes on J. N. D. Anderson's Life and Thought." *Al-Jamiah* 39, no. 1 (2001): 8–9.

—————. "Problem Gender dalam Perspektif Sejarah Hukum Islam." [Gender Problems from the Perspective of the History of Islamic Law]. *Nabila* 1 (1998): 14–26.

————. "A Problem of Methodological Approaches to Islamic Law Studies." *Al-Jamiah* 63, no. 6 (1999): iv.

————. "Reorientasi Kajian Ushul Fiqh" [Reorientation of Ushul Fiqh]. *Al-Jamiah* 62 (1990): 23–24.

————. "Supremasi Hukum dalam Masyarakat Madani: Perspektif Sejarah Hukum Islam" [The Supremacy of Law in Civil Society: History of Islamic Law Perspective]. *Unsia* 41 (2000): 23–33.

————. "Zakat dalam Konteks Otonomi Daerah." In *Tafsir Baru Studi Islam dalam Era Multi Kultural* [New Interpretations of Islamic Studies in a Multicultural Era], edited by M. Amin Abdullah, 211–36. Yogyakarta: IAIN Sunan Kalijaga-Kurnia Kalam Semesta, 2002.

Mohamad, Mahathir. "Islam Guarantees Justice for All Citizens." In *Hudud in Malaysia: The Issues at Stake*, edited by Rose Ismail. Selangor: Ilmiah Publishers, 2002.

Mohammad, Saifulizam. "Antara Hudud Allah dan 'Hudud PAS'" [Between the Penal Law of the God and the Penal Law of PAS]. *MASSA* (Malaysia South-South Association), nos. 13–19, July, 16–17, 2002.

Mortel, Richard T. "Madrasas in Mecca during the Medieval Period: A Descriptive Study Based on Literary Sources." *Bulletin of the School of Oriental and African Studies* 60, no. 2 (1997), 236–52.

Mudzhar, M. Atho. "The Council of Indonesian Ulama' on Muslims' Attendance at Christmas Celebrations." In *Islamic Legal Interpretations*, edited by Muhammad Khalid Masud, Brinkley Messick, and David S. Power, 230–41. Cambridge, MA: Harvard University Press, 1996.

————. "Dirâsat al-Ahkâm al-Islâmiyyah bin Mandhûur 'Ilm al-Ijtimâ.'" *Al-Jamiah* 65 (2000).

————. *Fatwa-Fatwa Majelis Ulama Indonesia*. Jakarta: INIS, 1993.

————. *Membaca Gelombang Ijtihad: Antara Tradisi dan Liberasi*. Yogyakarta: Titian Ilahi Press, 1998.

————. "Social History Approach to Islamic Law," *Al-Jamiah* 61 (1998): 78–88.

————. "Studi Hukum Islam dengan Pendekatan Sosiologi" [The Study of Islam from a Sociological Perspective]. In *Antologi Studi Islam: Teori dan Practice* [The Anthology of Islamic Studies: Theory and Practice], edited by M. Amin Abdullah, et al., 239–71. Yogyakarta: IAIN Sunan Kalijaga, 2000.

————. "The Ulama,' the Government, and Society in Modern Indonesia: The Indonesian Council of Ulama' Revisited." In *Islam in the Era of Globalization: Muslim Attitudes towards Modernity and Identity*, edited by Johan Meuleuman, 315–26. Jakarta: INIS, 2001.

Muhammad, Tengku Ahmad. "Dikir Barat Kelantan dan Kriteria: Perlukah Reformasi di Dunia Hiburan?" In *Seumbi*. Pulau Pinang: Planet Hijau Media, 2001.

Munir, Lily Zakiyah. "Has Shari'a Brought Justice?" *The Jakarta Post*, March 17, 2003.

Na'im, Abdullahi Ahmed An-. *Toward an Islamic Reformation: Civil Liberties, Human Rights, and International Law*. Syracuse: Syracuse University Press, 1990.

Nasution, Khoiruddin. *Status Wanita di Asia Tenggara: Studi Terhadap Perundang-Undangan Perkawinan Muslim Kontemporer di Indonesia dan Malaysia* [The Status of Women in Southeast Asia: A Study of Muslim Contemporary Marriage Law in Indonesia and Malaysia]. Jakarta: INIS, 2002.

Noor, Farish A. "Blood, Sweat and Jihad: The Radicalization of the Political Discourse of the Pan-Malaysian Islamic Party (PAS) from 1982 Onwards." *Contemporary Southeast Asia* 25, no. 2 (2003): 200–32.

———. *Islam Embedded: The Historical Development of the Pan-Malaysian Islamic Party PAS, 1951–2003*. Kuala Lumpur: Malaysian Sociological Research Institute, 2004.

———. "The Localization of Islamist Discourse in the Tafsîr of Tuan Guru Nik Aziz Nik Mat, Murshid'ul Am of PAS." In *Malaysia Islam, Society and Politics*, edited by Virginia Hooker and Norani Othmad, 195–235. Singapore: ISEAS, 2003.

———. "Reaping the Bitter Harvest After Twenty Years of State Islamization: The Malaysian Experience Post-September." In *Terrorism in the Asia Pacific: Threat and Response*, edited by Rohan Gunaratna. Singapore: Eastern University Press, 2003.

Nurhadi. "Muslims' Participation in Christmas Celebrations: A Critical Study on the Fatwa of the Council of Indonesian Ulama." *Al-Jamiah* 40, no. 2 (2002): 280–303.

Nyazee, Imran Ahsan Khan, ed. *Theories of Islamic Law: The Methodology of Ijtihad*. Perspectives on Islamic Thought, vol. 3. Islamabad: International Islamic University of Islamabad, Islamic Research Institute and International Institute of Islamic Thought (IIIT), 1994.

Osman Mohd. Taib. "Islamization of the Malays: A Transformation of Culture." In *Readings on Islam in Southeast Asia*, edited by Ahmad Ibrahim, et al. Singapore: ISEAS, 1985.

Othman, Mahmud Saedon Awang. "Islamic Law and Its Codification." *IIU Law Journal* 1, no. 1 (1989): 51–82.

Othman, Mohammad Redzuan. "Masjid Al-Haram dan Peranannya Dalam Perkembangan Awal Pendidikan dan Intelektualisme Masyarakat Melayu." *Jurnal Usuluddin* 13 (2001): 69–76.

———. 1994. "The Middle East Influence on the Development of Religious and Political Thought in Malay Society, 1880–1940." PhD diss., University of Edinburgh, 1994.

"The PAS View." In *Hudud in Malaysia: The Issues at Stake*, edited by Rose Ismail. Selangor: Ilmiah Publishers, 2002.

"Political Islam in Southeast Asia." Conference Report, March 25, 2003, School of Advanced International Studies (SAIS), Johns Hopkins University, http://www.sais-jhu.edu/programs/asia/asiaoverview/Publications/Southeast%20Asia/Political%20Islam%20Report.pdf (accessed October 2004).

Powers, David S. *Studies in Qur'an and Hadith: The Formation of the Islamic Law of Inheritance*. Berkeley: University of California Press, 1986.

Qodir, Zuly. "Wajah Islam Liberal di Indonesia: Sebuah Penjajagan Awal." *Al-Jamiah* 40, no. 2 (2002): 325–53.

Qu, Hong. "Impact of Islamic Family Law on Malaysian Muslim Women," http://www.asianscholarhsip.org/publications/papers/Qu%20hong-Impact%20%Islamic%20Familiy%20Law.doc (accessed October 19, 2004).

Rahardjo, M. Dawam. "The Kyai, the Pesantren, and the Village: A Preliminary Sketch." In *Readings on Islam in Southeast Asia*, edited by Ahmad Ibrahim, et al. 240–46. Singapore: Institute of Southeast Asian Studies, 1985.

Rauf, Muhammad Abdul. "Al-Hadith: Its Authority and Authenticity." *IIU Law Journal* 1, no. 1 (1989): 1–50.

Reid, Anthony. "Introduction." In *The Making of an Islamic Political Discourse in Southeast Asia*, edited by Anthony Reid, 1–16. Victoria: Center of Southeast Asian Studies, 1993.

———. "Perlawanan dalam Sejarah Naggroe Aceh Darussalam." *Tempo*, August 24, 2003.

Roberts, Robert. *The Social Laws of the Quran*. London: Curzon Press, 1924.

Saby, Yusny. "Islam and Social Change: The Role of the Ulama in Acehnese Society." PhD diss., Temple University, 1995.

———. "The Ulama in Aceh: A Brief Historical Survey." *Studia Islamika* 8, no. 1 (2001): 1–54.

Schacht, Joseph. *An Introduction to Islamic Law*. Oxford: Clarendon Press, 1964.

———. *The Origins of Muhammadan Jurisprudence*. Oxford: Clarendon Press, 1975.

Seng, Ann Wan. "Kenapa DAP Keluar Barisan Alternatif?" *Siasah*, November 2001.

Siraj, Mehruj. "Women and the Law: Significant Developments in Malaysia." *Law and Society Review* 28, no. 3 (1994): 561–72.

Sisters in Islam, "Letter to the Prime Minister," in *Hudud in Malaysia: The Issues at Stake*, edited by Rose Ismail. Selangor: Ilmiah Publishers, 2002.

Soetjoro, Sajid. "Tidak Cukup Dengan Pendekatan Keamanan." *Keistimewaan Aceh dalam Lintasan Sejarah: Proses Pembentukan UU No.44/1999* [The Special Case of Aceh in History: The Process of Forming Law No. 44/1999], edited by Kaoy Syah and Lukman Hakiem. Jakarta: Pengurus Besar Al-Jami'iyatul Washliyyah, 2000.

Stark, Jan. "Constructing an Islamic Model in Two Malaysian States: PAS Rule in Kelantan and Terengganu." *SOJOURN* 19, no. 1 (2004): 51–75.

———. "The Islamic Debate in Malaysia: The Unfinished Project." *South East Asia Research* 11, no. 2 (2003): 173–201.

Steenbrink, Karel A. *Beberapa Aspek Tentang Islam di Indonesia Abad ke-19.* Jakarta: Bulan Bintang, 1984.

Strawson, John. "Encountering Islamic Law." *Mimbar Studi* 3 (1999): 205–40.

Sudiyotomo, "ABRI Mendukung Penuh." In *Keistimewaan Aceh dalam Lintasan Sejarah: Proses Pembentukan UU No.44/1999* [The Special Case of Aceh in History: The Process of Forming Law No. 44/1999], edited by Kaoy Syah and Lukman Hakiem. Jakarta: Pengurus Besar Al-Jami'iyatul Washliyyah, 2000.

Sujitno, Sutedjo and Mashud Achmad. *Aceh: Past, Present, and Future.* Banda Aceh: Kantor Gubernur, 1995.

Suryadinata, Leo, et al. *Penduduk Indonesia: Etnis dan Agama dalam Era Perubahan Politik.* Jakarta: LP3ES, 2004.

Syah, Kaoy and Lukman Hakiem, eds. *Keistimewaan Aceh dalam Lintasan Sejarah: Proses Pembentukan UU No.44/1999* [The Special Case of Aceh in History: The Process of Forming Law No. 44/1999]. Jakarta: Pengurus Besar Al-Jami'iyatul Washliyyah, 2000.

Syirazi, Abu Ishaq Al-. *al-Luma fi Ushul al-Fiqh.* Cairo: Muhammad Ali Sabih, 1900.

Syurbashi, Ahmad. *Al-Aimah al-Arba'ah.* Beirut: Dar al-Jil, n.d.

Tambunan, Frietz R. "Pelaksanaan Syariat Islam: Sebuah Refleksi Berdasarkan Pengalaman Gerejan (Katolik)." In *Syariat di Wilayah Syariat: Pernik-Pernik Islam di Nanggroes Aceh Darussalam*, edited by Fairus M. Nur Ibr. Banda Aceh: Dinas Syariat Islam, 2002.

Tibi, Bassam. *Islam and the Cultural Accommodation of Social Change*, trans. by Clare Krojzl. Boulder, CO: Westview Press, 1991.

Tim Penulis Paramadina. *Fiqh Lintas Agama: Membangun Masyarakat Inklusif-Pluralis.* Jakarta: Paramadina dan the Asia Foundation, 2003.

Tiro, Tengku Hasan di. "Konsep-Konsep Kunci Ideologi Acheh Merdeka." *Suara Acheh Merdeka* [The Voice of Free Aceh] 7 (1995): 29–37.

———. "Nasionalisme Indonesia" [Indonesian Nationalism]. In *Mengapa Sumatera Menggugat,* edited by Yusra Habib Abdul Ghani, 41–67. Biro Penerangan Acheh-Sumatra National Liberation Front, 2000.

———. *The Price of Freedom: The Unfinished Diary of Tengku Hasan di Tiro.* National Liberation of Aceh Sumatra, 1984.

———. "Violations of Human Rights by Indonesia Acheh/Sumatra and Acehnese Legitimate Struggle for Independence from Indonesia." *AGAM: Madjallah Angkatan Atjeh Meurdeka* 4 (1991).

Wahid, Marzuki and Nurrohman. "Dimensi Fundamentalisme dalam Politik Formalisasi Syariat Islam: Kasus Naggroe Aceh Darussalam" [The Fundamentalism Dimension in the Political Formalization of Shari'a Islam: The Case of Nanggroe Aceh Darussalam]. *Tashwirul Afkar* 13 (2002): 34–57.

Weiss, Bernard G., ed. *Studies in Islamic Legal Theory,* Leiden: E. J. Brill, 2002.

Woodward, Mark R. *Toward a New Paradigm: Recent Developments in Indonesian Islamic Thought.* Tempe: Arizona State University, 1996.

Yasin, Norhamshimad Mohammed. *Islamisation/Malaynisatioin: A Study on the Role of Islamic Law in the Economic Development of Malaysia, 1969–1993.* Kuala Lumpur: Pustaka Hayati, 1996.

Yasuda, Nobuyuki. "Law and Development in ASEAN Countries." *ASEAN Economic Bulletin* 10, no. 2 (1993): 144–54.

Zain, Mohn Izani bin Mohammad. "Barisan Alternatif Selepas Tiga Tahun." *Minda,* June 2002.

ISLAM IN SOUTHEAST ASIA: VIEWS FROM WITHIN
Research Fellowship Program for Young Muslim Scholars

The fellowship program aims to enhance understanding of Islam in Southeast Asia from an "insider's perspective" while building the research capacity of young Muslim scholars and offering them publishing opportunities. Small grants are awarded annually for innovative research on issues concerning socio-political and cultural changes taking place in the diverse Muslim communities of Southeast Asia, especially as they relate to modernization and globalization. Key themes include: popular manifestations of Islam; shaping of Muslim identities in Southeast Asia by regional and globalizing forces; changing gender dynamics in Muslim communities; and the way Islamic values inform economic activities and social responsibilities.

Initiated in 2002, the program is managed by the secretariat of the Asian Muslim Action Network (AMAN) in Bangkok, Thailand, with the advice of leading experts from the region and the financial support of the Rockefeller Foundation.

Information on the program and how to apply can be found at
http://fellowship.arf-asia.org/

AMAN/ARF
House 1562/113, Soi 1/1
Mooban Pibul, Pracharaj Road
Bangkok 10800, Thailand

Tel: 66-2-9130196
Fax: 66-2-9130197

E-mail: aman@arf-asia.org
http://www.arf-asia.org/aman